IT'S TIME TO STOP PLAYING THE GAME!

The Black American Challenge of the 21st Century

Written and edited
by
Howard Bowens, Ph.D.
and
Jarrow Merenivitch, Sr.

in collaboration with

L. Patricia Johnson, Ph.D.
Anthony R. James
Melinda Horton

About the Cover

The cover of the book was chosen for its symbolic power. It represents the complex racial games that White and Black Americans play with one another. The book is careful, however, not to become seduced by this symbolism. Our primary focus will remain on the issue of Black peoples' survival. More specifically, we will focus on the type of vision, issues and "affirmative action strategies" necessary to assist in the process of Black American survival. At the same time, we will make frequent contrasts and comparisons between those strategies we have suggested for use by Black people and the visions, issues and "affirmative action strategies" employed by White people to promote their particular "self-interests." Some of the more innocent (or naïve) White people will have difficulty understanding the need or purpose for this type of comparative process. However, for those who are very skilled in using these tactics against the interest of Black people, there is no confusion.

The book cover was designed by Mr. Curtis McNair. We discussed the purpose of the book with Mr. McNair one afternoon and gave him a draft copy of the book to read. He then created the concept of the cover, and we are extremely pleased and grateful.

ISBN 1-58597-284-3

Library of Congress Control Number: 2004095301

LEATHERS
PUBLISHING

4500 College Blvd.
Overland Park, KS 66211
1/888/888/7696
www.leatherspublishing.com

Dedication To

L. PATRICIA JOHNSON, Ph.D.

It is with great respect and admiration that the authors of this book dedicate it to the memory of Dr. L. Patricia Johnson. Before her death, Dr. Johnson led a stellar and productive professional career. She was the Director of the Children's Division of the Georgia State Government in the administration of former Governor Jimmy Carter. In this capacity, she was responsible for a half-billion-dollar budget and over 5,000 employees. However, as impressive as this achievement might be, the true magnificence of this woman can only be understood through a variety of concepts that define her character. Dr. Johnson, or Pat to her friends, was a woman of immense integrity, courage, passion and conviction. Pat was resilient and resourceful. She loved people and was loved by them. It can be said that if Pat was your friend, you had a friend indeed because she possessed that rare quality of being able to express unconditional love. Pat was a consummate social worker, but she was also a strong leader who used her social skills to guide with wisdom and insight. In 1985, Pat made a statement that summarizes her philosophy of leadership and speaks to a fundamental principle underlying the thesis of our book: "The whole world cooperates with a made-up mind." We acknowledge and are grateful for the life of Dr. L. Patricia Johnson and for the significant role she played in the conception and completion of this project.

LIST OF CONTRIBUTORS

JARROW MERENIVITCH, SR.

Mr. Jarrow Merenivitch, Sr. is a retired Human Resources Executive. He retired from the Procter & Gamble Company after more than 32 years of service. He currently resides in Cincinnati, Ohio and is President of Creative Marketing Consultants, LLC. Mr. Merenivitch is vice-chair on the Board of Directors of Visions, Inc. located in Cambridge, Massachusetts. His career encompasses a wide range of experience in Human Resources Planning, Multicultural Organization Design, Management Development and Consulting. Mr. Merenivitch was co-author of the highly acclaimed action-research paper, *Toward a Multi-cultural Organization,* published internally by the Procter & Gamble Company.

HOWARD BOWENS, Ph.D.

Dr. Bowens is currently a Senior Consultant with Creative Marketing Consultants, LLC working out of St. Louis, Missouri. For the past seven years, he has been working as a community development consultant for College Hill Community 2000, Inc. in North St. Louis. Dr. Bowens' special project is the design and development of the exciting new concept of "Network Outsourcing". Dr. Bowens is a former assistant professor of management at Wayne State University. He has worked as an external and internal consultant to a number of organizations, including some ranking high among the Fortune 500. For many years his work has been concerned with the healthy integration and effective collaboration of the human resources in organization. Often, our lack of practical knowledge in the area of multicultural management creates organizations which are unhealthy for some people. This usually results in the loss of needed energy and contribution and, sometimes, it results in deliberate acts of sabotage. Dr. Bowens' dissertation and much of the thrust of his consultations over the years have been design to address the problems created by narrow cultural perspectives.

ANTHONY R. JAMES

Mr. Anthony James is President and CEO of Savannah Electric and Power Company, a position he has held since May 1, 2001. He joined Savannah Electric in June 2000 as vice-president of Power Generation and Senior Production Officer. Concurrently with his vice-presidential responsibility at Savannah Electric, James held a dual appointment as Central Cluster Manager for Georgia Power Company, a sister subsidiary of Southern Company. In this capacity, he managed five power generation facilities, ranging from one of America's largest coal-fired plants to a combustion turbine peaking plant located inside a major U.S. defense facility.

In 2004, James was selected as "Black Engineer of the Year" by *U.S. Black Engineer* magazine and Career Communications, a media services company that recognizes significant minority achievement in engineering, science and technology. He has broad experience in the areas of engineering, construction, power plant management, safety and health, corporate office administration, employee benefits and wholesale power marketing.

Prior to working for Southern Company, James was a resident engineer, a production department manager and an electrical and instrumentation manager for Procter and Gamble. It was during his tenure at Procter and Gamble that he developed the friendships with Dr. L. Patricia Johnson and Mr. Jarrow Merenivitch that led to his being one of the co-founders of Creative Marketing Consultants.

MELINDA HORTON

Ms. Melinda Horton is the Founder and President of Horton & Associates. She currently works as a freelance consultant for a variety of manufacturing organizations, primarily specializing in the high-tech and aeronautical industries. She received her bachelor's degree in 1961 from the University of Dayton and holds a master's degree from Cambridge University. Prior to starting her own consulting firm, Ms. Horton worked for many years as an internal consultant for Procter & Gamble, Paper Products Division, during which time she worked with and developed relationships with the other co-authors. Ms. Horton has also worked as an internal consultant for the Digital Corporation and has experience with nonprofit organizations.

What Time Is It?[1]

- A time to be honest with ourselves.
- A time to face reality, the "what is" in our communities and societies and still act with confidence and courage.
- A time to come together and collaborate.
- A time to face "Willie Lynch" and tell him that he is a lie.
- A time to return to the responsibility of raising and guiding our own children.
- A time to see life as the productive process of work.
- A time to end all excuses.
- A time to commit.
- A time to think, plan and act.
- A time, as always, to pray.
- A time to end the racism game.

---

1 In Chapter Three of the Book of Ecclesiastes, verses 1 through 8, there is a powerful thesis on the issue of time and timing. Our answer to the question posed here is that both the time and the timing is right in America to end the Game of Racial Dominance.

TABLE OF CONTENTS

PREFACE

This is a book about "Racial Games," the kind of games that have been played over the years and the games that are still being played to keep Black people *"in their place"* and away from the mainstream of American Economic, Financial, Social and Political success. The game was structured many years ago when certain advantaged White people realized that they could greatly enhance their wealth and their power by extracting free labor from African people. In the process, White people constructed a slave economy, a slave system to support the new economy and introduced ever-increasing numbers of Black people into the system. Once entered, Black people were never to emerge again as free human beings or spirits.

A very important part of the support and maintenance of this slave system was the physical characteristics, particularly the dark color of the African people who were sold into slavery. Since this characteristic was immutable, the person could be easily and forever identified as a member of the slave class and there was no avenue through which to escape, except by the grace and mercy of the white owner.[2] This strong color focus served the slave master well because his "property" could be easily identified and rebellion and escape attempts aborted. Color was paramount and a top priority. Through its use, the system of slavery could be secured. In addition, the different shades of color facilitated the creation of a perfect mechanism for dividing groups of slaves and preventing them from unifying with one identity and building group strength.

Now, in the 21st Century, many of the laws and codes that kept Black people in physical slavery have been repealed or shown to be unconstitutional and unenforceable. However, the *game* of using Black people as a major source of wealth through exploitation has not changed. One example is that the prison industry in this country is now one of its biggest growth industries. One could argue that Black people have only themselves to blame for this because they commit more crimes. However, all any reasonably intelligent and fair minded person has to do is examine the way laws are constructed and by whom and how the justice system around these laws is administered to understand why we include it as an example of continued exploitation of Black people for White peoples' gain.

Be that as it may, now that the laws that legalized the morally illegal behavior of slavery have been changed, the dominant culture has shifted to more subtle ways to hold Black people in check and to keep them in their *proper place*, a place they seem to believe is at their feet in eternal service to them and their children. The dominant culture now maintains its advantage because it has the power to structure the rules of "the life game" in America. White people dominate all the major institutions in this nation and, therefore, they are responsible for the criteria for selection, procedural operations, rules of engagement and evaluation. Instead of using physical force, Black people today are kept out of choice positions simply by orchestrating the requirements so that relatively few of them can qualify. One example shows the insidiousness in White people's determination to maintain control of an economic system they used free labor from Black people to help construct.

Whenever Black people try to introduce a serious program designed to remedy the ills they suffered from slavery, say the *reparations* movement to compensate Black people for their loss during slavery, White people vigorously fight it. One of the key weapons they fiercely use is the argument *against the use of color as a determining factor in the remedy.* They don't want color used as a factor in the hiring of or the selection of Black people for work positions or seats in a classroom. This remedy they call a *"quota,"* and they use this weapon to fight it as if their actual lives were hanging in the balance.

They don't want color used as the determining factor in the definition of *the protected class* or those who are slated to get *special treatment because,* just like the use of it in the process of enslavement, color is immutable. It is a clear demarcation that designates who is included and who is excluded from the class. Based on the historical record of the special treatment that White people were given during the period of outright discrimination and racial segregation, it would seem that color should be a major component in the process of identifying the people to be included in its remedy. However, what we find is that White people would rather use the concept of *minority group* to denote the protected classes.

The use of this more broadly inclusive concept allows them to water down the direct benefit Black people receive from any remedies by including almost every group in the country as a protected class. For example, the concept of *minority group* includes White women, who never experienced the race-based discrimination of Black women and who, throughout the system of slavery, went home to sleep with the White men who ran the system. It could, therefore, be said that White women obtained and enjoyed *collateral benefits* from the historic slave system. Now, through their inclusion as a *minority group*, they get special benefits from the remedy as well.

In the year of 2005, this country still has a long way to go to redress the ills against Black people that were set in motion with the first delivery of African Slaves in 1619. America could be much further along but the White power structure and the dominant White culture has been very successful in creating sophisticated *games* that keep the disparity between Blacks and Whites in all significant categories as wide as possible. It is the structure of these *games* that this book is designed to attack.

In order to defend ourselves from the array of energy-sapping games, Black people need to see the situation for what it is in reality. We are already human beings *endowed with the inalienable right to life, liberty and the pursuit of happiness*. We are already a *free* people in the sense that we have the *right* to go anywhere and do anything we please or that our checkbook will support. However, we are still very much enslaved in the sense that we have accepted or inculcated the Whites man's socially constructed reality of us instead of focusing upon our own self-interest and needs and living by a reality that we, as real free human beings, have to construct for ourselves. We are also enslaved because the "Willie Lynch Chip"[3] has successfully been firmly rooted in our collective psyches and the mentality that flows from it successfully destroys most of our attempts to act as a group upon our group self-interests.

Living in another group's construction of reality makes you tentative and weak. You are tentative because you are not quite sure if you have all the data you need to navigate the dangers that lay in the field. You are weak because the power of the system is based on a lifestyle, a language structure, a set of symbols and symbolic markers, a set of expectations, and patterns of behaving that are somewhat foreign to you. When Black people engage with White people in a social setting, the differences in some of the areas mentioned above are immediately noticeable. The problem, however, is not that there are differences. The problem is that all of the standards for quality and excellence that are set for these differences are based upon White cultural criteria. In every area, Black people are measured against White people's cultural values. The result is that we are perceived to be inferior when we use our own cultural set and marginally successful when we use the White standard.

Okay, if this is the problem, what is the solution? The solution is very simple to state but extremely difficult to bring into reality. The solution is for Black people to realize that we really are living in the 21st Century and not in 1619. We are living in 2005 and not 1950 even. If we could really believe that we are living in the 21st Century or fool ourselves somehow into believing it, we would simply behave as the free men and women we are. We would behave just like White men and White women. What does that mean? It means that we would feel free to perform the jobs we are given to the best of our ability, using the skills that we possess and that have been developed through our particular cultural experience. It means that if we are in charge of recruiting for a major company in America, and we happen to be Black, we would do our job to the best of our ability, which is to say that we would find and hire as many qualified Black people as there are openings in the company.

White people, through the use of the "Degrees of Me" philosophy that will be discussed later, do this for their friends and associates all the time, but then explain the lack of Black representation on the *difficulty of locating qualified Black applicants.* The sad fact is that we as Black people generally accept this lame excuse for failure as the best that White people can do. It is not their best performance. It is failure, plain and simple, and any Human Resources Manager who can't do his or her job and find the few qualified Black people their company has requested to fill positions should be fired for incompetence, not given a pass because *"they did the best they could."* Another way of saying the same thing is to say that Black people need to assist White people in correcting these weaknesses. We need to help them end the games we have been playing with each other for far too many years.

If you look at any game structurally, you will find that it has a group of components that holds it together and makes it what it is. Take away any of those components and the game changes, sometimes significantly. If we were to view the games played between Black people and White people as a two-party or two-player game, one thing becomes crystal clear. The *only way* the game can be played and enjoyed is for *both* parties to play their respective parts according to the rules that have been established. If *one* of the parties ceases to play in accordance with the established rules or stops playing altogether, the game is over at that point. For example, take the game of tennis. If you and I are playing this game and I refuse to hit the ball back to you when you serve it to me, the game is over. It simply cannot be played without my consistent cooperation.

Although it will not be easy, this is the *one strategy* that will put an end to the years of racial gamesmanship that Black People and White people have been playing in this country. Just stop hitting the ball back. If Black people were to simply focus 110% of their energy and effort on projects that are designed to promote their own group's self-interest, White people would have to go find someone else with whom to play their dominance game. We would be too busy planning and constructing the new, high-performance reality we want to live in the future.

This is a different, perhaps even strange, way to look at life because Black people are so used to and comfortable with the game of *social ping pong* that supports White domination in America. They say, for instance, that we are not qualified, we then react with complaints of discrimination and demonstrations. They try to keep us out of their neighborhoods and we try to do everything we can to get into them. They act and we react, they serve and we return serve. That is a ping pong game and it is the actor who has the advantage. What would happen if you simply didn't hit the ball back and you responded this way no matter how many times they tried to get you to play? Instead, you decided what you want and what goals you wanted to achieve and you put *all* of your time, energy, focus, emotion, talent and experience into achieving those objectives. That is where we are headed with this book.[4]

Whether we actually get there or not is dependent upon

whether we are successful in our objective of showing or revealing the weaknesses in the system of racial games we have been playing in this country for years. Assuming that we will accomplish this objective, we hope that the book will encourage every Black person and every fair-minded White person to end the games by ceasing to play the submissive roles that are required to keep the game going strong.

---

2 In the Virginia Colonies, slave owners instituted a practice known as "meritorious manumission." In an effort to thwart organized or planned attempts to revolt or escape, the owner would promise immediate and total freedom to any slave that told them of such plots and prevented an escape.

3 For a much fuller examination of the Willie Lynch situation review the article—"Honor thy Father and thy Mother but Kill Willielyntology" reprinted in the Appendices.

4 The reader should know that the main principles that are discussed in this book are currently being applied in a long-term community revitalization process in the College Hill Neighborhood of North St. Louis, Missouri. College Hill is a majority African American community that has suffered the brunt of strategic disinvestments for a number of years. The revitalization process has been underway since 1996 and is beginning to show evidence that the approach is practical, relevant and successful.

INTRODUCTION

While this book has a rather broad scope, it is relatively specific and narrow in its purpose. In scope, the book will touch on such general themes as *Unity,*[5] *Racial Healing, "Affirmative Action," Internalized Oppression, Racism, Dominance and Subordination, etc.* It will demonstrate, in the words of Cornell West that "Race Matters" in America.[6] It will also attempt to show why it matters. We will address such issues as how race has mattered historically; how it mattered in the creation and continued maintenance of the dominant white status quo. We will offer a rationale not only for why it is likely to continue to matter but why it *must* matter as we look to the successful resolution of race issues in the country's future.

Race in America has traditionally been a source of divisiveness. For this reason, we acknowledge that it is a little risky for us to say that race *must* be considered as we discuss and search for ways to improve our ability to manage the interactions among the races. But, as suggested in the opening section, America is a "pluralistic society"[7] with respect to race and it has always played a major role in this problem. The literal fact is that differences in color are an ever present reality in our society. Historically, there has been differential treatment of light-skinned people over dark-skinned people in every institution of this American Society. We may not like the unintended associated negative implications of this fact but the historical reality remains the same. Race and color differences have mattered and still do matter in America.

As Black authors, speakers and professionals, we want to make our contribution to the ongoing effort to build and achieve a truly multi-cultural society.[8] Exhortations by some people that this society should be "color blind"[9] while often noble in intent, fail to acknowledge the important place that *race* and *color* have played in building the economic strength of our nation.[10] Once the country had become strong by utilizing race and color to force slave labor to build it, race and color continued to play a vital role in denying Black people any just reward for their labor or an ability to compete for a better position. These concepts have also been important factors in the continued maintenance of the dominant White social and economic hierarchy that exists today.

We are rapidly approaching a situation where the masses of Black people will no longer be needed or considered useful as a source of raw labor. Now that color is no longer an exploitive economic benefit in this society, some people want to talk about the society becoming "color blind." But, to argue that the severely unequal playing field, which was created by an "immutable race and color focus," could realistically be leveled without taking race and color into account is ludicrous. It is naïve (at best) and purposely deceptive (at worst) to deny the fact that White people have historically enjoyed and still enjoy a distinctive and pervasive "color-based advantage" in this country.[11] Race does matter in today's America! Given this reality, our book makes an honest attempt to discuss ways in which race has been used to play the "dominance game" and many other games. We will discuss and bring to light some of the ways race matters as a way to reduce some of the negative effects. We believe in the Biblical principle that understanding is a crucial element in the process of problem resolution.[12]

Although, as we have said, the book is broad in scope, its central purpose is narrowly directed. Its purpose is the ending of the insidious, energy-draining, non-productive and destructive games that are played between Black and White Americans. There are blame games; denial games; race card games; and games which utilize the legalism of specific language to proclaim a personal innocence for the creation of the problem. There is the institutional racism game. There is the game of "no controlling legal authority." This game causes people to emphasize what is legally correct to the exclusion of the morally right thing to do. And, there is the "variety of code words for Black people and black issues game." All of these games are played daily in this country as we each go about pursuing our conception of the illusive idea that is called "The American Dream."

The discussions in the book will be similar to holding an open "Black Town Hall Meeting" where we will address our particular issues (in America) from our own unique perspective while others are allowed to silently listen. This approach, that is, the approach of opening the discussion to allow some vicarious participation by White people, has some validity because we know that the particular problems associated with the fact that "race matters" in America cannot be solve by Black Americans alone. We are only one element in the game. However, at the risk of overemphasizing the point we made earlier, there is one important fact often overlooked in the dialogue between White people and Black people with respect to "games" and the operation of the "racial equation." Games are very fragile structures once you really examine and understand them.

To play and maintain any game requires that the participants follow certain prescribed rules and that they cooperate with at least a minimum set of behavioral expectations. Since this is true, it follows that it is also true that all two-party games (individual or group) can be altered, or completely terminated by one party's refusal to follow the designated rules. When attempting to reduce racial gamesmanship, it is often difficult to get either party to accept the responsibility for the continuation of racial adversity or for their conscious decision to "play the game." For this reason, it is hard to reach a place where we can relax our guard and reduce the gamesmanship.

Our book accepts this reality. But we still step forward

to say what we believe is needed is to end or kill the game. From such a perspective, this book may be viewed as either a "request" for interested White Americans to stop playing their part of the game, or yet another "wake-up call" to Black Americans stressing that it is imperative that we stop playing our part. For our own survival, Black people have to learn to critically examine the game, to review the rules of play and to stop playing the "*mass media scripted roles*" that contribute to our own destruction. If we (Black Americans) do nothing suggested in this book except devise and implement strategies designed to defeat the vestiges of the law of "*Meritorious Manumission,*" the authors would be satisfied. This law was established in the Virginia Colony in 1710. If we do something to nullify its effects, we will have finally taken a major step toward the objective of breaking the bars of our "mental imprisonment."[13] We will have stricken a critical blow to one of the structures that attacks the relational connection among Black people and that makes effective group collaboration almost impossible.

Since, as we have said, Black Americans are only one part of the game, the contents of the book will also contain information about some things that White Americans can do. However, we want to be very clear about the limitation in the focus of this book. White Americans, as the dominant cultural group, control all the major institutional power resources in this country, be they economic, political, educational, legal, communications media, entertainment, industrial, etc. As a Black American minority subculture, Black America cannot be assured that any White person will see, be interested in or do anything to resolve the problem on their end. That is why our main focus in this book will be on the issue of the survival of Black Americans in the midst of America's process of evolution from a dominant "monocultural (Eurocentric) society" toward a more fully multi-cultural society.

An essential part of the main objective of the book requires a clear, well-constructed and documented discussion of a few basic issues. We want to highlight some of these points prior to discussing them more fully later:

1. The re-telling[14] of our traditional, historical story.
2. The insidious phenomenon of "Meritorious Manumission[15]" as it was applied during our enslavement.
3. The military tactic of "wounding[16]" an enemy to reduce fighting capacity and to create dependency for the purpose of exploitation.

(1) The notion of re-telling our historical story is presented with an example in Chapter Two. The story must be told in such a way or manner that causes us to focus more on the exploitation of our fore parents' free labor than on the moral horror (and supposedly guilt producing cruelty) of forced slavery. Black American slaves were a fundamental building block (a "corner stone") in the creation of the economic wealth of this country. A truer story is that, far from a picture of Black people having contributed little to the value of this country, the nation was built upon the strong backs of Black people. A primary resource for documenting this argument is Dr. Claud Anderson's *Black Labor, White Wealth: The Search for Power and Economic Justice.*

The history component is the foundation of our book. It is very important but it is also tricky. Black slaves had little control over their use or treatment. The review of this history causes a burning sensation in the emotions of Black readers but our focus must remain upon how the historical reality is connected to the "games and issues" we face today. The current toxic reality of dominance and inequality was an "orchestrated inequality." This must be revealed because if we are going to address the reality effectively, we must acknowledge it and see it for what it is. White people may continue, if they so choose, to "play the game of denial of the historical facts" but Black people don't have to continue to waste our energies "playing the supportive game of begging them to stop the denial." There is a better use of our time, energy and effort. We must utilize our talent and energy to dismantle the structure of racism with all its institutional supports.

(2) The "Peculiar Institution" of American Slavery had an insidious but highly effective nature. The effectiveness of this institution was influenced by three factors. First, was the factor of its particular and random brutality. Second, was the denial of any rewards for labor. Finally, there was the use of race and color as definitive and immutable characteristics of class, privilege, and personal worth in combination with the use of the power of religious, legislative, legal and educational institutions to create acceptable rationales for the exploitation. As if this were not enough, slave owners instituted a type of scientific brainwashing process begun in the Virginia Colonies (1710) under the name of "Meritorious Manumission."

This highly effective process has created an almost permanent group of "wounded people" who can be continually exploited for economic advantage because of the "crabs in a bucket" effect of this training. It drastically curtails and sometimes prevents the development of interpersonal trust, an ingredient so necessary for productive group cohesion. Today, Black people provide the basis for a number of major new growth industries to employ members of the dominant class. For example, academicians and other intellectuals earn both money and status by studying Black people and becoming experts on our plight. Black male and female convicts comprise nearly one quarter of the country's population but one half of the prison population and, thereby, support a law enforcement system that is becoming one of America's best growth industries. There is also the welfare system. On the plus side, it is responsible for feeding children and providing health care for needy individuals. However, it also bears responsibility for containing regulations that required the absence of the father and prevented the single mother from legally obtaining other supplemental work income without losing benefits from the program. The unfortunate negative side effect of the requirements weakened the Black family unit and helped ensure the continued availability of needy Black people to sustain the employment of other members in the society. In fairness, family deterioration may not have been an intended outcome of the program designers, but it has clearly become one of the results.

(3) The notion of "growth industries" sustained by "wounded" Black people is very important to our ultimate purpose because it suggest that there is the opportunity, however remote, for Black people to begin to build step ladders that will help us climb out of the situation. We can begin to develop small businesses under our control that are sustained by the natural production of our people. We realize that, in some cases, it is a distasteful notion to think of raising your family on income created by the controlled wounding of your own people but the reality already exists. It is exactly what is happening with much of the social services industry such as Welfare, Empowerment Zones, Medicaid, etc. The income and livelihoods that are generated by these programs are based upon the existence of large numbers of wounded Black people. And, these programs support huge bureaucracies of middle class, suburban-dwelling, tax-paying, affirmative-action-hating White males and females and their families.

This book is structured to provide two separate but interdependent kinds of knowledge: 1) knowledge for understanding and 2) knowledge for action. While individually necessary, neither by itself will help us very much. One body of information is the history (knowledge) of the background of the current situation. Without knowing what has been done and how it has been applied, we cannot effectively counteract the negative impact. Although personally incensed by the principle of "Meritorious Manumission" and the speech delivered by Willie Lynch in 1712,[17] we realize that the deed is done. At least we can say that the information from Mr. Lynch did us a service by articulating the elements of the process. The brainwashing system won't be easy to eradicate but we do have a fighting chance.

The second body of information is data for action. We must use strong, consistent, directed and "*offensive action*"[18] focused on the weaknesses of a seemingly impregnable fortress of White privilege. We almost have a situation that is similar to the members of the Massachusetts 54th, that proud contingent of Black soldiers featured in the movie *Glory* who volunteered to be the first group to attack the Civil War fortress of Fort Wagner. These proud Black soldiers were fully aware that they would not win the battle. They knew they were in a "mess." However, they also knew that they had earned the right to call themselves men. They had earned this right because they were prepared to *ante up and kick in*. This, essentially, is the same challenge that faces every Black person currently living in America today. The question is still squarely before each of us: *"Are you willing to ante up and kick in?"*

We conclude this introduction with a personal story that might appear at first glance to be an unnecessary aside. The experience happened to one of the authors during a trip to Washington D.C. to attend an information conference for the Harvest Institute.[19] Our colleague was walking past the various foreign embassies that are spread around Connecticut and Massachusetts Avenues in Washington, D.C. One of the most impressive was the Embassy of Japan. After admiring this magnificent structure, he walked back toward the hotel. Near the intersection of Decatur and Massachusetts he had a momentary "spiritual insight."

At this intersection there was a brief encounter with a

well-dressed, clean-shaven Japanese businessman. The two passed each other on the sidewalk. Our group member nodded his head in pleasant greeting. The Japanese businessman moved his head in acknowledgment but continued to look straight ahead. The event might have gone unnoticed except for the expression on the face of the Japanese businessman. It was an expression that signaled an encounter with someone who was of little significance, consequence or importance. Our member could just as easily have been a tree instead of another human being. Then, the insight came. Realizing that he could have been mistaken in his interpretation of the experience, the member took time to enter the insight into his diary as a note to himself. It was a note in answer to a self-query concerning why he had been even remotely disturbed by this man's lack of acknowledgment of another human being. He wrote:

A man (or woman) won't respect
You until You respect Yourself.
You, however, won't respect Yourself
Until You do something to earn it.
And, remember, only a fool
Will lie "to" Himself or Herself
"About" Himself or Herself.

From that moment on he became committed to a decision to *do something*, to act in every area of his life in a way that earned his respect for himself. Part of what we are saying in this book is that it is time for us, for all Black people, to examine this same question and to decide to do something for ourselves to earn our own self-respect. It is time to *ante up* in some fashion and *kick in* some effort. It is time to focus upon what we need to do for our people and, then, to **DO IT!** The final item we want to present are the inspirational words from a totally unexpected source. The words were discovered on the same trip to Washington and during the same walk that resulted in the personal "spiritual insight." The words were engraved on a large and impressive statue of a man named Tarus Shevchenko. We have taken the liberty to reprint the inscription here:

DEDICATED TO
THE LIBERATION, FREEDOM AND
INDEPENDENCE OF ALL CAPTIVE NATIONS[20]

This monument of Tarus Shevchenko 19th Century Ukrainian Poet and Fighter for the Independence of Ukraine and the Freedom of all mankind, who under Foreign Russian Imperialist Tyranny and Colonial Rule appealed for "The New and righteous law of Washington," was unveiled on June 27, 1964. This historic event commemorated the 150th anniversary of Shevchenko's birth. The memorial was authorized by the 86th Congress of the United States of America on August 31, 1960. And signed into Public Law 86-749 by Dwight D. Eisenhower, the 34th President of the United States of America on September 13, 1960. The Statue was erected by Americans of Ukrainian Ancestry and Friends.

— Leo-Mol, Sculptor
— Radoslav Luk, Architect

On a separate (also huge) concave slab located to the rear of Mr. Shevchenko's statue were his own prophetic and inspirational words:

... Our soul shall never perish.
Freedom knows no dying,
And the greedy cannot harvest
fields where seas are lying:
cannot bind the living spirit
nor the living word.
Cannot smirch the sacred glory
of th' Almighty Lord.

— *Taras Shevchenko, The Caucasus, 1845*

---

5 A very important distinction is made in the conclusion of the book regarding the concept of "unity." We draw the distinction between "The Spirit of Unity" and "The Unity of the Spirit." It is the second expression, "The Unity of the Spirit" that best characterizes the spirit that informs what we have written in this book.

6 Cornell West, *Race Matters* (Boston: Beacon Press, 1993).

7 Harold Cruse, *Plural, But Equal* (New York: Quill-William Morrow, 1987). There are many references that document the notion of America as a plural society. We highlight Dr. Cruse's work because it discusses the important additional idea of the "equality in America's plurality."

8 Multicultural in our sense is represented by a large round table where all of the cultures in our country are present in equal status. Each is contributing the fruit from their culture to enhance the American scene.

9 Arthur Schlesinger, *The Disuniting of America* (New York: W.W. & Company, Norton, Inc., 1993).

10 Claud Anderson, *Black Labor, White Wealth: The Search for Power and Economic Justice* (Edgewood, MD: Duncan & Duncan, Inc. Publishers, 1994).

11 An exercise conducted by Dr. Andrew Hacker reveals the real perceived value of "Whiteness." The exercise required White students to place a monetary value on their "Whiteness" once they learned that a mistake

had been made at their birth documentation and now they must live out the next 50 years of their lives as a Black person. The monetary value these students placed on their "Whiteness" is very revealing. Dr. Hacker discusses this experiment in his book *Two Nations: Black and White, Separate, Hostile, Unequal* (New York: Ballantine Books, 1993).

12 God inspired the wise writer of Proverbs to write— *"Get wisdom, get understanding: forget it not; neither decline from the words of my mouth. Forsake her not, and she shall preserve thee: love her, and she shall keep thee. Wisdom is the principal thing: therefore, get wisdom: and with all thy getting get understanding."* Proverbs 4:5-7(KJV).

13 For a brief description and explanation of "Meritorious Manumission" see page 166-167 of Dr. Claud Anderson's brilliant work *Black Labor, White Wealth.* Also see our "Honor Thy Father and Mother but Kill Willielyntology" article in the Appendices.

14 We owe the notion of "re-telling" our history in this manner to the work of Harlan L. Dalton. His book, *Racial Healing: Confronting the Fear Between Blacks and Whites* (New York: Doubleday Dell Publishing Group, Inc., 1995) is a must read if the reader is to appreciate the importance of the idea. His brief account of the usual way we tell our story is compelling to us if not to the White people to whom we tell it. We received permission to reprint this account in our book so that the reader can understand that while it is important to re-tell the story factually, it must be characterized in another way.

15 Anderson, Ibid. (Pages 166 & 167). This relatively harmless sounding concept is the basis for a most profound type of psychological enslavement. In 1712, a man by the name of William Lynch had crafted the principles of this program into a model of "conditioning" which he went around selling to slave owners. His speech is contained in the article "Honor Thy Father and Mother but Kill Willielyntology" in the Appendices. The article is a "working paper" written by one of the co-authors to suggest a strategy that may help "deprogram" Black people from the effects of this early form of "scientific social engineering."

16 This is an extremely important concept for Black people to grasp. We will attempt to document that Black people in America have been "wounded" by the policies and practices of this nation and how this "wounded status" has been and "is being" used to continue to fuel the American economic engine today with almost the same effect that slavery had in times past.

17 See the essay "Honor Thy Father and Mother but Kill Willielyntology" in the Appendices section.

18 See the paper entitled "Offensive Tactics Against Covert Racial Discrimination" reprinted in the Appendices.

19 The Harvest Institute is a new Black "Think Tank" located in the Nation's Capital. The institute was founded by Dr. Claud Anderson,

author of *Black Labor, White Wealth: A Search for Power and Economic Justice.* The primary goals of the institute are:

To design and promote a national policy, with prescriptive solutions to bring about economic and political self-sufficiency and competitiveness.

To establish new forms of institutional leadership.

To link knowledge to power by bringing together scholars, strategists and researchers.

To establish an electronic information network within Black America.

To promote accountability, unity and optimism.

The Harvest Institute is a non-profit, non-partisan, tax-exempt 501(c)(3) organization. It is located 1244 - 19th Street, Washington, D.C. 20036. The phone numbers are (202)-496-1624 & Fax (202)-496-1624. Please consider *The Harvest Institute* when looking to invest your future tax exempt charitable contributions.

20 Interesting! Here stands a monument dedicated to a Russian Freedom fighter, authorized by the 86th Congress and signed into law by Dwight D. Eisenhower, at a time which was near the height of our cold war with Russia (The Union of Soviet Socialist Republics).

— Chapter One —

VOICES CRYING IN THE WILDERNESS

One of the most well-known historical experiences of "voices crying in the wilderness" is the Biblical account of the Israelite people who, after spending 400 years in captivity, wandered another 40 years in the wilderness on their way to the "Promised Land." Black people also spent a long time in outright slavery to the "citizens" of a developing American nation. Since the passing of the 13th Amendment, which ended the legal justification and support for slavery, Black people have been wandering in another kind of wilderness on the way to the promises of this land.

In 1865, when Black people were released from the servitude of slavery, America promised our people 40 acres and a mule. America promised Black people equal opportunity and equal access to education. America promised Black people fairness through its constitutional principle that, "All men are created equal and endowed with certain inalienable rights." America promised Black people the right to, "life, liberty and the pursuit of happiness." And as Pharaoh did with the Israelites of the Old Testament, America promised that it would, "Let our people go."

America kept part of its promise by removing the physical chains of servitude, but it "let us go" not to the land of its promises, but to a modern day style wilderness. This is not a natural wilderness of desert, of barren terrain or of hostile environmental elements. America created a new wilderness of psychological servitude and despair born from state-supported systems of segregation, educational neglect, discrimination, Black Codes, and Jim Crow Laws. The country allowed brief periods of political, legal and civil gains that were quickly followed by periods of legal retractions of those gains. The net result has been to keep Black people wandering aimlessly in frustration and confusion and to keep their focus away from the actual achievement of what America promised.

This issue was the concern that first brought our group of experienced consultants, teachers, administrators and corporate executives to the Eastman Room of the Best Western American Hotel, Atlanta, Georgia. We each were "survivors," if you will, of the Black wilderness experience. We had become trained professionals with over twenty years of struggle and achievement in the American business environment. As survivors of this experience, we have decided to take the opportunity to document some of the learning gained from our journey and to make a sincere attempt to communicate what we have discovered.[21]

As we now enter the early part of the 21st century, we find that Black people are still living in the wilderness that has been constructed by America as a way to keep us from the "Promised Land." Historically, there have been many "cries" from this wilderness; cries of pain, cries of anguish, cries of outrage. We now add our voices to the many others who have been *"crying" in this "wilderness."* However, this is not a cry of despair. It is not a cry of hopelessness. It is a cry of encouragement and confidence. It is a cry for mobilization and readiness. We believe that Black people are poised on the shores of the land of promise. It is our responsibility to take control of our destiny, to focus on the promises that our foreparents earned with their blood, sweat and tears and to take the actions required to achieve their dreams.

In the 20 to 30 years the writers have spent trying to achieve effective assimilation in American society and to make contributions to corporate performance, we have learned many lessons. Some of the important lessons are distilled in the brief points that follow:

1. The waters may be calmer now than during the period of slavery but make no mistake, there is still real danger out there. This point was expertly driven home by a Black executive speaking at a reunion of a group of Black managers who worked for a progressive Fortune 500 company. The speaker was part of a panel of successful alumni of a plant within this company and he was providing some tips from his experience to younger Black managers. His advice to them was poignant, "Don't ever take off your gas mask."[22]

2. You can win! We may not have achieved all of the success we deserve or would like, but there are clear examples of success and the chance for us to succeed. As with the Israelites who were facing their promise land, there may be reports of "giants in the promise land," but we can take the land and claim our promise.

3. You have a birthright, which is your responsibility to reach back and help someone else progress even as you were helped. It is a sobering reality, but no less a reality, that the time it is going to take to neutralize some of the destructive effects of racial separation and discrimination will likely span the current readers' entire lives as it will ours. But, we are part of an historical process of change and we must do our part to push it along even though we may not be around for the big reward ceremony. We must understand that we are part of an historical context and that our common historical experience creates a collective self-interest, a destiny that we must accept, appreciate and fulfill.

4. It takes a special kind of courage and strength to remain

> diligent in the face of the challenges that confront us in this "orchestrated wilderness." However, it is not courage or a strength that we do not already possess. It takes the kind of strength that has almost been raised to an art form by Black women in America. *There is a kind of strength that is almost frightening in Black women. It's as if a steel rod runs right through the head down to the feet. And I believe that we have to thank Black women not only for keeping the Black family but the White family ... Because Black women have nursed a nation of strangers. For hundreds of years, they literally nursed the babies at their breast who they knew, when they grew up, would rape their daughters and kill their sons* (p. 10).[23]

The real message in all of this is that the "promises" are still there. They exist even while we are in our psychological wilderness, just like the "*Promised Land*" existed for the Israelites even while they were lost in a physical wilderness. Reflecting on the Israelite experience is instructive because, through it we realize that, in order to possess the land of promise, this band of former slaves had to take some very specific action. For example, they had to "believe" the promise. They had to fight the demoralizing doubt and sense of hopelessness of their people that had kept them circling in the wilderness. They had to organize themselves for the collective purpose of securing their promise; they had to act in the specific interest of obtaining the things that God had already promised them.

Black people appear to have these same challenges as we stand at this point in history, in the morning of a new millennium. This book represents our acceptance of the challenge facing every Black person. We are choosing to step forward and contribute what we believe we know. In this book, we present what we have learned from our real-life experiences as consultants and managers in the corporate halls of America and in general life in American society.

In accepting the challenge of this book, we are aware that we face some legitimate criticism when the limitations of our perspective confronts the different but, likewise, limited perspective of some of our readers. We have found it necessary on occasion to make some bold, declarative statements in this book, statements which may seem unjustified, inaccurate, and even unfair given the experiences of other readers. This is unavoidable. It is excusable, however, because it is exactly the same problem any group of writers must face when attempting to conceptualize and communicate what they know from their experience to an audience comprised of people outside that unique experience. What we believe, however, would be inexcusable on our part, is to produce a piece of work addressing such a complex topic which purported *not* to have this limitation. No amount of data, regardless of how scientifically it is collected and analyzed, can substantiate a value-laden perspective based on a person's or group's particular experience in a culture. We have had too much of that sort of thing already and it is another type of "game" we would like to end.

While the general subject of this book is *diversity* and the creativity and productivity that can flow from a process of integrating and *managing diversity,* the book project itself is the result of a process of *diversity management.* Each of the authors has experience that is unique in some way. We come from different age and gender groupings. We are from different professional backgrounds. We were raised in different geographic localities and have different socioeconomic backgrounds. Yet, while there is considerable diversity among the members of our group, we have struggled to collaborate. This project is the result of an earnest pooling of our experience, research, thinking and writing. In a single document it represents the synthesis of our individually unique knowledge bases, a coming together in a passionate ensemble of our singular voices in chorus. Such a synthesis is, in and of itself, significant. We have collaborated in the production of this book in the very way that we believe companies all over the world will need to collaborate if any of us is to meet the opportunity presented by the global economy expected in this 21st Century of world history and beyond.

To succeed in our task, we had not only to acknowledge the diversity of backgrounds, perspectives and skills among us, but we also had to show an appreciation for these talents by demanding that they be brought forward and applied to the task at hand. Everyone in the group had the responsibility to guard the process from those sneaky, subtle attacks that stem from our own bag of "isms" — sexism, elitism, regionalism, ageism, etc. The lack of diligence in this area is a major factor in the destruction of many collaborative efforts.

One of the major issues in the *management of diversity controversy* is discovering a way to overcome the parochialism and shortsighted partisan divisiveness that stem from cultural/racial separation. But, this difficulty is not a product of *racial diversity* alone. Similar problems are experienced every business day as a result of the parochial views that tend to develop from functional specialization. Success in the racial diversity arena could have major implications for breaking down the other dysfunctional walls that hamper cooperation and communication in American business organizations.

A second point of significance, while related to the first, is more important. We view ourselves as concerned representatives of the African-American culture. We are all Black professionals. Thus, we bring to the table knowledge, skills and talents acquired from our involvement as Black professionals in White corporations. We also bring to the table, unfortunately to our own detriment, a set of negative experiences that have worked to destroy the effective collaboration of Black people for many years. These are the negative effects that stem from the ravages of *internalized oppres-*

sion.[24] These effects don't evaporate because we consider ourselves friends or because each of us has some identifiable self-interest in this project. As a developing team, we had to face these divisive factors directly and to remain vigilant in watching for their subtle, negative influence throughout the collaborative process.

During this project, there were forces that rose to divide us. However, we were unified by one common thrust, one common passion that drove us to complete the task. It was the passion to have our experience in this country as Black professionals make a difference to the world. To try, if you will, in the words of some immortal soul, "… to be part of the solution to some of the problems we face in the area of multicultural management rather than be part of the continuation of those problems." We believe that our learning in the area of *diversity management* is not only a contribution to the world but it is one of the major personal gains from this project.

A final clarification is required before we enter into the body of our discussion. The concept of diversity, as it is commonly used today, has undergone a peculiar evolution. Say the word "diversity" out loud today and you will conjure up a host of concepts that have somehow been fused together to mean the same thing (e.g., *cultural diversity, affirmative action, multiculturalism, globalism and minority issues* to name just a few). In the book, we address this confusion directly, particularly with regard to the *coloring of a concept* idea that is discussed in Chapter Three.

As a conclusion to this chapter, we want to say a word to our colleagues in the great academic institutions of our country. We trust that some of them will find an occasion to read this book. However, the book was written for a different audience. Although we believe our analysis is consistent with the data that has come from years of systematic, empirical research, much of the data we present will fall into the category often referred to in academic circles as *anecdotal*. Usually, when this term is used by academics, it is intended to diminish the seriousness and value of the information, at least, as it is compared to the "data" produced by "controlled, quantitative, empirical research."

We acknowledge this criticism and respect the contributions of the research tradition out of which it flows. However, despite such criticisms, it has been our experience that when the results gained from carefully controlled experimental designs are used to enlighten or improve actual business practice, the method often selected is one that we might call *logical anecdotal association.* In other words, it involves a similar use of anecdotes to effectively communicate a conclusion or a summary point.

For all African Americans, like ourselves, who must use our knowledge in very practical "messy" situations, we believe the data in this book will prove especially useful. None of us are able to divorce ourselves from these issues. We do not have the option of separating ourselves from the specific social problems that are the substance of this book. Such issues are an integral part of the normal developmental patterns of our lives here in America. As we watch the shrinking of our world as evidenced by global competition, the lightening like acceleration of our communication and information storing and retrieving technology, we may very well be able to assert that *multiculturalism* is our society's only chance of surviving the perils of our future.

We see some real danger for America if she ignores or is simply incapable of mustering the will to effectively manage *the process of diversity* toward *true multi-culturalism.* The racism game must end. We truly believe that the information and perspectives in this book can be useful to all people who choose to actively respond to the diversity challenge in this country. Since it is unlikely that White people will step forward to initiate this effort, Black people must take the lead. We are the ones who must earn our livelihoods, live our lives and raise our families in this country.

We are the ones who have to work through some pretty hostile corporate cultures. Therefore, Black people will do well to use the information in the book as an army uses its intelligence reports. The information in this book can be used as a guide to help Black people analyze the societal and corporate terrain, avoid the "land mines," and make effective contributions of their talent while they survive the many threats to their psychological, physical and mental health.

---

[21] See the article in the Appendices entitled "Stemming the Tide of Black Professional Suicide: A Call for Point People." The article makes the point about the responsibility of Black professionals to help end the game by acting as effective "point people" who prepare the way and warn of danger.

[22] This quote was delivered by one of the former Black managers during a session at the reunion of Black managers for the Procter and Gamble Paper Products Plant located in Albany, Georgia.

[23] Excerpted from R. Williams, *They Stole It But You Must Return It,* P. 10.

[24] Internalized oppression is that psychological condition where the person being oppressed by a system actually internalizes and accepts the negative characterizations and stereotypes of them.

— Chapter Two —

A BRIEF HISTORICAL OVERVIEW: WHY DO WE HAVE THE RACIAL GAMES THAT WE PLAY?

The philosophical thrust of this chapter follows the prescription of Dr. Harlan L. Dalton as presented in his book *Racial Healing*. Dr. Dalton suggests that one thing that Black people need to do, as part of our contribution to the notion of racial healing or improved race relations, is to re-tell the Black historical story. We must tell it accurately but in a way that more specifically relates the history to present-day realities. As a refresher, Dr. Dalton first articulates a brief but fairly comprehensive synopsis of the way the historical story is usually told. We reprint his synopsis for the convenience of the reader and so that we might make our point more clearly:

> *We were brought to this continent in chains, physically enslaved, deprived of all freedom, and subjected to continuous abuse. Our culture was suppressed, our families ripped apart, and our women raped. We were deliberately kept ignorant, and were prohibited from learning to read or write. Our attempts to rebel were brutally crushed. Despite all this, we survived as a people, developed a strong culture of resistance, and endured.*
>
> *When we were eventually emancipated, we did not*

become truly free. Even our emancipators had no interest in embracing us as equals, and we lacked the knowledge and resources to create a world of our own. Our only choice was to remain subservient.

The era of Reconstruction – society's effort to help us get on our feet – was altogether too brief, and was followed by a long period of bondage by another name. Slavery was replaced by Black Codes and Jim Crow Laws. The slavemaster's whip was replaced by the lynch mob's rope. Legal advances were often ephemeral, and were offset by grandfather clauses, literacy test, and outright intimidation. "Separate but equal" was the law of the land, and somehow only the first part ever got enforced.

When legal segregation gave way in response to agitation from Black people and their White allies, de facto segregation took its place. It continues to this day in much of daily life. Once formal segregation was ended, the Civil Rights Movement took on discrimination in employment, housing, and public accommodations. After a series of legislative and judicial victories, backlash and retrenchment set in. New barriers were erected. Suddenly, progress for us was seen as a form of "reverse discrimination." Meanwhile, those Blacks who did manage to enter the mainstream discovered that it was less than hospitable.

On a related front, we began in various ways to explore and assert our distinctive cultural identity. We looked to our African roots for inspiration in art, music, history, rituals, and even the names we gave our children. We paid attention to our hybrid African-American culture, and developed ways of giving it expression. We had scarcely begun when a cultural backlash set in. In many quarters, nationalism and multiculturalism came to be seen as sinister, and as an attempt to impose political correctness. Suddenly,

White males were being hailed in the press as America's true victims.

While we were struggling on all these fronts, the economy underwent a sea change. Manufacturing jobs and entry-level jobs in other fields with prospects for advancement were nowhere to be found. Unskilled and semiskilled jobs have fled overseas. Even as formal racial barriers come down, we are stuck at the bottom with no place to go. In many ways, Black men have become an endangered species. With no way to provide for families by legitimate means, the lure of easy money on the street, and the availability of addictive substances to dull the pain, we risk losing an entire generation to the nation's prisons and jails, to drugs and to AIDS.[25]

We were hesitant to use this traditional historical synopsis because, as Dr. Dalton says, "*This narrative is quite compelling, and is a powerful reminder of the difficult road we have traveled together as a people.*" As we remember and revisit our history, we become aware of a couple of apparent dangers in the historical story as uttered above.

One danger is that it pulls upon the worn-out guilt strings and diminishing moral indignation of White people. As more and more time passes, White people have less feelings of guilt and more feelings of anger because they see Black people continuing to "blame" them for the "*sins of their great and their great-great grandfathers.*" White people were not the victims of the color-based, forced slavery system and they don't personally suffer in the present from any of its residual effects. Therefore, it is almost impossible for them to really identify, emotionally, with the pain. To expect White people to personally relate to such a story is self deception.

The second danger in the story is that it is emotionally wrenching to Black people, whose great and great-great-grandparents were the victims of the horrors and who still suffer from lingering residuals that have been institutionalized into the fabric of our society. The result is that some of us are paralyzed by rage and lose the ability to stay focused upon the structural elements that support and maintain the system. As we re-tell the story in this chapter, we will take care to focus attention upon the relationship of our history to the key survival problem of Black people today. We do not intend to minimize or ignore the emotional impact or true horror of our history in this country but we must ensure that the knowledge of the history helps us understand the present reality. We must do this so that we can act to effectively change it or act to protect ourselves from the negative things that we cannot change.

Like Dr. Dalton's account, our historical account is not intended to be a comprehensive discussion of the foundation of racism in the United States. It is rather a broad sketch of historical events in order to describe the basis for the philosophical perspective of the book. The historical points are important primarily because a main objective of the book is to shift the paradigm of Black readers away from a focus on the emotional horror of the historical trek of Black people in this country. Our intent is to examine these events for their economic consequence and, therefore, to become more aware of the economic impact of the vestiges of this history in the society of today.

In the United States, the *diversity phenomenon* as we know it today is an artifact of the long-term historical processes set in motion early in the seventeenth century with the decision to bring African slaves to this country to help facilitate its economic development. Following the Emancipation Proclamation, up to and including the first part of the 1950s, America was immersed in a stage of *stark segregation.*[26] This *stark segregation* stage was represented by the blatant, overt denial of opportunity to Black people. It was not uncommon, even in the mid 1950s, to see employment advertisements which clearly specified that "Negroes need not apply," regardless of any specific qualifications they may have possessed. During this period, Black people were segregated by custom, historical stereotypes and *negative assumptions about their ability and value.*[27]

While there was some pressure through small activist movements working to change these patterns, significant and sustained change was not to come until the Civil Rights Movement of the 1960s. During this period, a type of moral consciousness surfaced and the development of early equal employment opportunity legislation made it more difficult to foster blatant acts of segregation and discrimination.

At this time, it became necessary for business establishments to remove the evidence of overt discrimination. Recruiting and advertising materials began to carry the now familiar notation: *"We do not discriminate on the basis of race, color, creed or national origin."* But policies regarding gender discrimination remained largely unstated and, consequently, unchanged. However, it is interesting to note that later attempts to redress the discrimination against women that had been based upon the immutable biological characteristic of their gender were included under the category of "minority"[28] rather than "gender." Women, especially White women in America, were not discriminated against because of their "minority status." Therefore, the inclusion of White women within the specific classification of "minority" has drastically diluted the available resource pool for addressing the problems experienced by people of color because of the biological characteristic of their color.

Merenivitch and Reigle refer to the period of civil rights gains as the *"nondiscrimination phase."* This phase represented a passive approach to the cultural change, cultural integration problem. Companies seemed to be saying that the removal of blatant discriminatory policies and advertising language would, by themselves, make everything all right. However, as a consequence of this passive approach, very little change occurred in the organizational makeup.

The blatant signs of overt discrimination had been reduced, but Black people and other ethnic employees continued to receive treatment inherently different from and less than that received by their White counterparts.

Then, in the early 1960s, as a result of the lack of real progress made under passive, nondiscrimination corporate policies, the federal government initiated a more active, aggressive set of programs. The program known as Affirmative Action had "action" as its operative concept. It instituted a set of accountability standards with respect to goals and timetables. In the view of Merenivitch and Reigle, these programs initiated the *Affirmative Action Generations* that they divided into two sequential phases, as detailed in Figure 1. The most important contribution of their work is the notion that each of the two phases or generations was associated with specific issues that characterized an organization's position on the historical, developmental continuum of multicultural diversity management.

Merenivitch and Reigle's conceptualization of the *affirmative action debate* as phases through which organizations develop is extremely important for the question of African-American survival in the general business organizations and corporate structures of America. Assuming that progress in the area of diversity management is naturally slow, Black people caught in organizations that still have policies, procedures and people who are unfavorable to them, have to possess the knowledge and skill to survive long enough for the slow, subtle changes to take place. At a minimum, they have to have a way to determine the place or stage their organization is located on the diversity developmental continuum.

Additionally, they have to be able to predict the kinds of behaviors to expect from a particular stage and their potential effect upon them and their career. This is an entirely different focus from the more common approach of hunting for organizational racists or trying to discern who is a bigot.

Figure 1

THE PROGRESSION OF THE GENERATIONS OF AFFIRMATION ACTION TO MULTICULTURALISM*

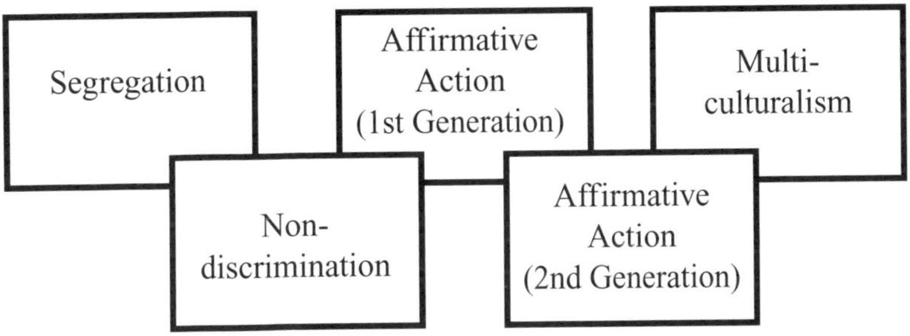

The diagram above illustrates the progression of organizations from the stage of segregation to multiculturalism. The two generations of Affirmative Action are distinguished by the issues that prevail during each generation:

First Generation

Focus on numbers
Crisis orientation
Resistance to proactivity
Social issues
Racial & sexual hostility
Trust
Technical competence
Evaluation
Upward mobility
Involvement & accountability
Dual roles
Fear of backlash
Sex and color blindness
Sex and color exaggeration
Isolation of Affirmative Action

Second Generation

Critical mass
Racism and Sexism are dead
Residual stereotypes
Retention & career development
Career disillusionment
Implementing accountability
Role of White male managers
New backlash issues
Legitimization of racial issues
Constituency
Racism vs. Sexism
Affirmative action & org. devel.

* Used with permission of the authors.

This approach recognizes the institutional, structural aspects of racism. It, therefore, involves a more strategic analysis of the kinds of organizational inputs that cause or support the behavior that can be expected from organizations at a certain level of diversity development. Such a focus gives Black people an opportunity to plan for a more strategic response that would enhance their personal survival within the particular organization.[29]

As we write this book, we stand at the dawn of the 21st Century. However, we find ourselves in a position very similar to that of Merenivitch and Reigle as they wrote. We, too, are writing about a process at one point along the developmental continuum. From this position, we can reflect upon and speak accurately about events that have occurred in the past but we can only speculate concerning the events of the future. As we move into the next few chapters, we will engage in two distinct activities. One is reflection. The other is prediction.

But, before we move on, it is important to summarize two major points that stem from our perspective on Black history. The first point is that the reality of race relations today is the result of a long evolutionary process that has become far removed from the objectives that were the bases for its origin. In the early17th Century, White entrepreneurs contemplated the use of African slave labor in the context of "economic opportunism." The dismantling of Black families and the systematic dehumanization of Black people were processes that evolved in complexity as slave owners tried to manage and maintain this system of free labor. The book, *The Slave Master: The Ideal in Slave Management in the Old South* by James O. Breeden, is a chilling account of the efforts of slave owners to apply "scientific management" principles to the system of slavery. The accounts are all the more chilling when one realizes that the authors of these ideas were probably the more educated and benign of practicing slave owners.

The second point is that the experience of Black people in America, for the most part, has been the result of a *grand social experiment.* We know that the development of Black people as we stand today was a very long evolutionary process. It is also clear to us that, even when not consciously intentional, this was an "orchestrated evolution." Often, in the past, when White Americans were confronted with programs designed to redress social injustices done to Black people, they objected to what they felt was an attempt at "social engineering." The statement, "You can't legislate morality," was frequently uttered in response to such corrective programs. However, the existence of the slavery system and the maintenance of many vestiges of that system today represent examples of "social engineering" in actual practice on a massive scale.

While some people may view it as implausible to attempt to "legislate morality," the existence of the slave system and its residual effects reveals that it was not implausible for White people to construct and implement a system that would in effect "legislate immorality." In the book *Psychology of the Black Experience* (1972), Black psychologists writing in the early 1970s state the issue in the following manner:

> *The importation of Africans as slaves to this country constitutes the greatest known mass manipulation of human beings for the purpose of molding their behavior to comply with pre-determined criteria. Therefore, in another sense, the history of the Afro-American has constituted the greatest social-psychological "experiment" of all time, when the conditions of the experiment were not in whole or in part self-imposed.*[30]

These writers make the point that we have gone to great pains to legislate a society which regulates Black people to "biological inequality" in direct conflict with a fundamental precept underlying the foundation of this nation, *"We hold these truths to be self-evident."* Information contained in the chapters which follow will help the reader gain a better perspective on the effects of this "orchestrated inequality."

---

[25] This entire section is reprinted from *Dalton's Racial Healing,* pp. 150-152.

[26] This section follows Merenivitch and Reigle, 1979. The labels given to the stages are theirs. We have included a reprint of their original work in the Appendices.

[27] We will discuss this issue more completely in Chapter Six during our exploration of the "Deficit Model" as one of the eight barriers to true multiculturalism.

[28] We have placed the term "minorities" in quotes here to highlight an important point which will be explained in more detail in a later chapter concerning the confusion that seems to be deliberately created around the selective use of certain concepts. In the area of race relations, "minority" began as a concept which simply meant that Black people and other people of color were citizen populations whose census numbers were less than the "majority" White population. As various economic programs have been developed for these groups to redress the negative effects of past discrimination, the concept of "Minority" has been expanded to include an array of other groups (e.g., White women, other peoples of color, gay men and women regardless of color in some cases. More recently, there have even been attempts in certain circumstances to include White men who are not gay if their numbers are in the "minority").

[29] See "Offensive Strategies in the Face of Covert Racism" in the Appendices.

[30] Psychology of the Black Experience.

— Chapter Three —

THE FIRST GENERATION OF AFFIRMATIVE ACTION

Before we move into a discussion of the vital concepts of the *Generations of Affirmative Action,* we have to take some time to clarify our use of the term *Affirmative Action.* This clarification task is perhaps the most important and the most difficult communication objective in the entire book. As we prepare to approach the clarification task, we are aware that even the notion of clarification is fraught with hurdles that threaten its very intent.

What is it, specifically, that we want to clarify? There is not a simple answer to this question. For one thing, we want to clarify our point of reference with regard to some of the important but common terms used in this book. Terms such as "multiculturalism," "minority," "affirmative action," "cultural diversity," etc., are a few examples. One aspect of the problem that should immediately become obvious is that these terms are already loaded with meaning that stem from their common everyday use in our society. If we intend, as we do in the case of *affirmative action,* to suggest a slightly different meaning or emphasis, we run the risk of creating even more confusion instead of enhancing the goal of clarification.

However, we must make the attempt because a common understanding of some of the terms currently used in the discussion of diversity issues in the United States is crucial to the main thesis of this book. In this sense, if we are successful in communicating our point with respect to the confusion over some of the important concepts, we will be able to both expose a major game and avoid the problems associated with the game at the same time. The game is the language game and, while we often say that "the devil is in the details" of a plan, the real devil is in the definitions of its key component parts.

We believe, as demonstrated in the previous chapter, that the current and very complex issues of race in the United States were initiated with the historic and, primarily, economic decision to use forced African labor to develop a productive economy for this country. Over time, these issues have undergone their own evolution through a variety of subsequent decisions that produced a variety of social and political structures to justify the economic institution of slavery. Finally, the vestiges of these justifying belief systems and the subtle institutional practices that sustained them over time still remain as formidable barriers to any changes that challenge the status quo of "Eurocentrism" in this country. In order to make meaningful progress toward more diversity within major corporations and in the nation, we must focus upon what has occurred in this country to maintain a system of advantage that has been partly built upon human misery. We must understand what some of the barriers are and something about the nature of the processes that currently support them.

One of the most subtle, yet extremely powerful processes that has prevented the successful correction of past inequities is a strategy we will refer to as the *coloring of a concept.* Through this strategy, the majority White controlled media have been able to use the enormous communications machinery at its disposal to control the meaning generation process and the interpretation of commonly used terms.[31] The *coloring of a concept* idea addresses a very effective technique used in the media to systematically associate negative, dysfunctional or even disaster events with the color *Black* and, by association, to Black people. Through this seemingly innocent process, the media have been able to nullify or alter the dictionary meaning of certain concepts simply by relating them to Black people. A few examples of innocent concepts that have been "colored" in this manner should help to illustrate the point we wish to make — *Quota, Busing, Welfare, Affirmative Action,* and even *Minority.*

Utter any one of these familiar words today in the context of an interracial discussion and they will either stir a lively debate or stop the conversation altogether. The technique of changing positive or neutral concepts into negative ones through an association to issues of Black people has clearly worked. The only thing that people who want to use this mechanism need to do is relate a concept often enough and long enough to Black people and the term loses most of its general and positive meaning.

One of the examples used above is the concept of *Quota.* Before the concept was "colored" through its association with Black people gaining "unfair advantage over White people" in things like college admissions and job selection, White people used it all the time. It is still used frequently in the context of sales and marketing with few negative connotations. In addition, the concept of "quota" has a long established use by the majority culture to regulate the number of immigrants allowed into the country, especially the number of people of color.

The concepts of *Bus* and *Busing* are another example. The familiar "yellow bus," before being associated with desegregation programs, was a sign of a good school system engaged in the normal behavior of transporting happy kids to their normally rural or suburban schools. During the height of desegregation orders to redress past discriminatory practices, White people reacted to the idea of "busing" as if the whole transportation industry had been created to bring unqualified Black children into their neighborhoods.

It is interesting to note that, while the original bus transporting of White children in rural school districts continued during the desegregation period, the negative connotation of the term "busing" was only used to refer to the transportation of Black children to White schools, or vice versa, on those occasions when it did occur.

Even though the coloring of the term "busing" was bad, without parallel, the gravest and most detrimental use of this subtle technique has been the "coloring" of the concept *affirmative action.* The success of White people's attack on this concept threatens to end what some have referred to as the "Second Reconstruction." The genesis of the affirmative action concept can be traced to the early 1960s. In March 1961, President John F. Kennedy signed Executive Order 10925 and created the President's Committee on Equal Employment Opportunity.[32] The Executive Order "brought the phrase *affirmative action* into common usage ...." Here is the wording from the order:

> *"The contractor will not discriminate against any employee or applicant for employment because of race, creed, color or national origin . . . [and]* ***will take affirmative action*** *to ensure that applicants are employed, and that employees are treated during employment, without regard to their race, creed, color, or national origin."*[33] [emphasis added]

When read in its context, it is clear that the intended use of the concept *affirmative action* was as a kind of modified verb. It simply described the kind of behavior that would be necessary to correct the overt discriminatory practices that had traditionally been applied to deny Black people equal treatment in comparison to White Americans and equal access to the employment opportunity in this country. Contractors were instructed *to take affirmative action* to ensure that applicants are employed, and that employees are treated during employment, without regard to their race, creed, color or national origin.

The true spirit of the order was intended to pressure those employers who took advantage of government support to take positive or "affirmative" action to hire and develop employees who had been systematically excluded from employment opportunity prior to the order. Affirmative action for Black people in this context was necessary because White employers had historically taken affirmative action to ensure that Black people would *not* be employed. As previously stated, some business employment advertisements, as late as 1954, carried the bold disclaimer, ***"Negroes need not apply."***

Therefore, as can be seen from the wording of the actual order creating the concept, *affirmative action* was intended to convey the kind of positive action that would rectify past discrimination in employment and treatment of American citizens who were not members of the dominant class. However, laws and executive orders can be circumvented in others ways. Rather than the modified action verb intended by the order to redress past practices, the term has been drastically altered through its association with negative consequences that are then connected to Black people. The majority class has used its control of the media to turn the concept of *affirmative action* into a kind of *sinister noun* that they broadly define as *any method, program or idea that discriminates unfairly against White people in favor of Black people.* The concept has been successfully "colored" through the use of this technique. It has lost nearly all of its intended positive behavioral effect and has even been abandoned by many Black people who see it as a concept that is almost synonymous with *special treatment* for them.

It is important for us to emphasize that the specific concept of affirmative action is not the problem. The term in and of itself is value neutral in that it means to *act affirmatively.* It is the power exerted through the majority class's control of the "meaning making institutions" of America which has altered the neutrality of the concept by marrying it to Black people and embodying it with the negative images they often associate with Black people. These are images such as "getting something for nothing," or "the lowering of standards," or "the selection of unqualified Black people over better qualified White people." All of these negative images can now be induced by the simple use of the concept affirmative action.

The attempt to explain the subtle tactic of creating negatives through association, particularly as it relates to the concept of *affirmative action,* is important even if the clarification is unsuccessful. It is important because affirmative action does relate to actual behavior that was either taken or not taken to correct historical employment problems for Black people. In order to prepare Black people for survival in American business organizations, it is necessary to be able to determine what the environment or culture is and how to evaluate any potential threats that may exist to their well being.

We have chosen to stick with the concept of *affirmative action* in its original meaning as contained in President Kennedy's executive order. We do this because *affirmative action* is not a concept that applies only to Black people to the detriment of White people. It is a concept that describes all behaviors that are systematically applied to a situation in order to change its reality from one state to another. If the executive leadership of major organizations were to think of the concept in this fashion when focusing upon racial issues, they might understand that it involves a process that is very similar to the way executives approach most of their other organizational challenges. However, since we are not sure if key White executives will ever be able to make this kind of shift in their thinking, it is necessary in this book to provide Black people with a way to use the concept of affirmative action to evaluate an organization's culture relative to them so that proper decisions can be made.

To help facilitate this result we not only stay with the affirmative action concept but we have also utilized the Merenivitch and Reagle idea of *Affirmative Action Generations.* This unique conceptualization allows us to separate the environments of organizations that have "acted" proactively to do something about the problem from those that have not done as much or have mainly "reacted." In the remainder of the chapter, we characterize the key behaviors that typify an organization at certain stages along a development continuum of affirmative action progress leading to a fully diverse, multicultural entity.

First Generation Affirmative Action Issues

Merenivitch and Reigle listed a variety of issues that were confronted in the First Generation of Affirmative Action. Here, however, while we will review these issues we will limit our discussion to those issues that we feel are the most relevant in characterizing this particular developmental phase and in helping to provide the foundation for success and survival of Black people in organizations.

(1) Focus on Numbers: One of the primary issues characterizing the First Generation is the concentration on numbers. The corporate emphasis in the 1970s was on recruiting and initial promotion of minorities and women to first and second level management positions. Numerical goals were based on the government's minimal required standards and there was little consideration of what was needed to normalize the participation of minorities and women in the organization. To quote Merenivitch and Reigle, "There was often a collective sigh of relief from the top management of an organization that was on target with regard to its numerical goals."

This emphasis on "counting heads" can still be witnessed

today in organizations or organizational units where representation is low. However, in the wake of the dismantling of the accountability standards for affirmative action programs during the decade of the 1980s under President Ronald Reagan, the collective sigh of relief is not heard so loudly. While organizations cannot return to the blatant discrimination of the "stark segregation" phase that preceded affirmative action, there is less motivation today for First Generation firms to push forward toward the Second Generation stage.

In 1979, Merenivitch and Reigle discovered one negative implication of the numbers focus of the first generation. They found that it could lead to "suspicions and fears of potential charges of reverse discrimination and legal suits." We now know that escalating fears, suspicions, charges of reverse discrimination, and actual litigation have been associated with *affirmative action* activities. So much confusion and conflict occurred during the decades between the 1970s and the 1990s that the very mention of the term affirmation action would conjure up emotions of hostility, especially when there was suspicion of the use of the latest addition to the *subversive list of un-American activities* — the infamous *quota.*

The existence of these reactions to affirmative action is real, as real as the fall of the Berlin Wall. However, in our view, these reactions are less associated with the existence of affirmative action programs than with the "conscious negative mismanagement" of the programs as cultural change processes. For example, in the early phases of an affirmative action program we often heard comments, in defense of a hiring or promotion decision involving a woman or minority such as, "We had to or were forced to do this by the government"; or "Our hands were tied, Joe, on this one." The implication underlying such statements is that the *only* reason to promote a minority would be legal pressure. This implies that actual ability to perform the job had little to do with the choice. The sad part of the commentary is that we don't have to listen very hard in organizations today to hear these same types of justifications being offered.

Why do we associate these reactions with "conscious negative mismanagement"? Inescapably, it is the responsibility of an organization's management system to ensure that it has the material and human resources required to maintain and improve the organization's productivity. Blaming bad human resource decisions on governmental regulations that a manager believes are detrimental to the accomplishment of organizational goals is irresponsible. It is worse than irresponsible to imply that you "picked a man off the street" to do a job when, in most cases, the person selected met at least the minimum standards set for performing the required duties.

The disturbing part about the admissions by some managers and supervisors that they were forced to choose "x" or "y" minority because of *affirmative action* is that it appears somewhat out of balance with reality. While some managers or supervisors find it easy to refer to *affirmative action policies* as the reason for certain personnel selections when it involves people of color, it is almost impossible to get them to admit to *affirmative action* with respect to majority employees. For example, very little is said about the affirmative action taken when an otherwise qualified female employee is not selected for a high level position because, "We were afraid that she would not be accepted by or fit into the male golf circuit." A similar case occurs when an otherwise qualified Black professional is not promoted because, "We were concerned about the potential negative reaction of his white peers."

We say that this situation is out of balance because a refusal to admit such occurrences reinforces the myth that selections of White employees are always based upon talent and objective analysis while minorities of color need preferential treatment through affirmative action. There is very little willingness to admit to the affirmative action taken in the favor of Whites people to maintain the dominant status quo.

One of the structures for white affirmative action involves the use of "floating criteria." This is a concept we will examine in Chapter Six as an example of one of the major barriers to an organization's achievement of multiculturalism.

(2) Crisis Orientation: Organizations operating within the First Generation of Affirmative Action tend to use a *"crisis orientation"* with respect to their response to issues that arise between racial and gender groups or individuals within those groups. Merenivitch and Reigle accurately identify a situation where problems of a racial nature have to be overt and acute in their implications before the organization is stimulated to act. They report that the absence of such a crisis leads to a "why-do-anything syndrome" which is partly reinforced by the orientation to numbers.

We have already said that the main impetus for action by organizations in this developmental phase is the compliance/legal focus. Such a focus tends to gauge the need for action on the existence of crisis situations such as volatile emotional exchanges, strikes, discrimination, violence, charges or legal suits in progress. The basic feeling seems to be captured by the notion — "If we aren't getting Equal Employment Opportunity (EEO) charges or open confrontations, we must be in an acceptable position."

First Generation organizations tend to be reactive. More than simply being reactive, however, they aggressively seek to resist proactivity. There is a "collective fear" that proactivity will cause or create problems; a fear that close examination of problems or opportunities in this area will create more or worse problems. The result is either a "Catch-22" or a "self-fulfilling prophecy." Failure to manage proactively the integration and processes of assimilation of *minorities* predisposes the organization to generate the very problems that it believes the inaction will avoid. This is somewhat like failing to change the oil in an automobile for fear that we might not be able to reseal it properly, thus losing the new oil and ruining the engine. As with the warning in the old familiar Fram Oil Filter commercial, "You either pay me now or pay me later."

The other side to "only reacting to crisis" is the wish to "avoid creating a crisis." Consider the following hypothetical situation. Suppose a company has had a good experience in locating suitable housing for its professional personnel in an attractive suburban subdivision with quality schools and easy transportation to the work site. Suppose that, over time, good relationships develop among the working professionals and the organization begins to realize an additional performance benefit from the cohesion and communication fostered through common participation in non-work activities such as neighborhood clubs, PTA meetings, car pools, etc.

Now insert a few talented Black professionals into the same network of formerly all white professionals. The company may find itself unwittingly pulled into a racial quagmire. The attractive subdivision has been a happy home for most of the white professionals but it may not be eager to accept Black people as residents. Realizing that it cannot blatantly discriminate against Black people, the management of the subdivision chooses to use a number of delaying tactics designed to frustrate the applicants into seeking residence elsewhere.

What should the company do? While the organization truthfully can say that it is not in the housing business, it is also true that, historically, the organization encouraged the other professionals to seek residence in this area and other professionals living there freely offered information and assistance to other candidates. It just happened that, until now, all of the other candidates were White. What should be done? What will be the consequence of doing nothing to assist these black professionals? Is assistance "preferential treatment," especially, since "nothing" had to be done for White professionals? What will happen if the Black professionals choose to fight or make an issue of what appears to them to be obvious discrimination on the part of the subdivision's management? Should the company support the Black professional's fight?

While the situation above is hypothetical, it is easy to see how it could, without any intent by anyone, stir up an issue of racial conflict. It typifies the dilemma for a First Generation Affirmative Action organization. Such a situation could cause a major problem for a company in the First Generation Affirmative Action Phase because of the tendency to ignore the larger natural issues that arise due to the social changes implicit within cultural, racial, or gender diversity.

(3) Uneasiness About Race and Gender: Merenivitch and Reigle highlight a number of issues in the discussion of their First Generation which reflect a tenuous uneasiness of organization members in dealing with issues involving race and gender. The uneasiness, however, is reflected over a very wide range of expressions from open hostility to the utter denial of any influence of race or gender. It is true that some of the same behaviors discussed in this section can be found in the Second Generation of Affirmative Action but it is a question of frequency and degree.

In the First Generation of Affirmative Action, it is not uncommon to experience openly expressed hostility on the part of male employees toward female employees and of White employees toward Black and other minority employees. It is also true, even if it isn't overtly expressed, that a similar hostility is generally felt by women and minority employees toward the "generic White male oppressor." Much of the hostility on the part of the White male majority in organizations is expressed through subtle negative racial innuendo , overt racial slurs, sexual jokes, labeling and open discounting. These occurrences are not viewed by the perpetrators as *racism* or *sexism* and, therefore, when challenged, the hostility is denied — "I didn't mean anything by that" or "Can't they take a joke?" etc.

Simultaneously, there is the existence of a "sex and color blindness" and a "sex and color exaggeration." This is a real challenging paradox. On the one hand, there is a tendency to deny or be blind to the idea that race and gender have anything to do with specific interpersonal or performance problems. For example, as highlighted in the previous section, when moving a Black manager to a new plant located in a White community, the organization may be blind to the potential negative effects that the normal process of finding suitable housing may have on his or her performance. In a similar sort of blindness, the resistance to a woman's managerial authority may not be factored into performance reviews even though she has been assigned to take charge of a crew, unit or department that never worked for a woman manager before.

At the other extreme of this paradoxical situation, race and gender may be exaggerated as factors contributing to interpersonal difficulties, performance problems, or promotion advantages. For example, a conflict between a Black employee and a White employee may be viewed as being caused solely by race, with other possible contributing factors being ignored. With such a narrow focus, the organization may fail to recognize general problems — such as inadequate training or career development programs — that affect others in the work force as well as the minorities and women.

One of the most unfortunate outcomes of the "Uneasiness About Race and Gender" in the First Generation is that it creates a "fear of backlash" type of reaction that interferes with organizational performance. In this developmental phase, there is a pronounced fear of "White male backlash." There are a couple of reasons, however, that provide some insight into or basic understanding for the existence of these feelings. First, the strong focus on achieving "the numbers" creates a feeling that the organization's standards have been lowered and that minority men and women have been given *unfair advantage* because of their race and/or gender.

A second cause of the "fear of backlash" reaction is that racial and gender problems are normally defined in First Generation organizations as "we-they" problems rather than as issues of a collective responsibility. Under such a philosophy, the fear of adverse reaction from Whites is offered at every step in the change process as a reason for not making changes that will result in greater equality of opportunity. Instead of confronting and managing adverse reaction as part of the natural resistance to change, the organization slows down or stops affirmative action planning. A major concern of the organization's leadership becomes the pace of change — "How fast can we or should we go?"

(4) Low Sense of Organizational Legitimacy: The unfamiliarity, newness, and tenuous work relationships between Whites and minorities and between men and managerial level women of the First Generation produce a fair amount of doubt and mistrust. Whites, Blacks, men, women, and other minorities find themselves working together but holding conflicting views and feelings about the legitimacy of the relationships. For example, White male managers may not seriously believe that minorities and women constitute legitimate professional peers. The most common feeling, if not openly stated, is that women and minorities "have only made it as far as they have because of *affirmative action.*"

There is skepticism concerning the ability of minorities and women to succeed in some (if not all) types of positions. Women and minorities are assumed to be less capable than White males and, when they happen to prove otherwise, there is a feeling of surprise. One result of these attitudes is that women and minorities tend to be kept in staff or support roles longer than equally qualified White males before being given the opportunity for an operational assignment where they have to exercise authority over others.

Another variation on the same theme is to give minorities leadership positions that were traditionally perceived as part of the fast track only when those positions no longer hold the same importance in the politics of the corporate climb. This lack of balance in the experience and exposure of women and minorities is not generally viewed as a problem because very little serious attention is given to the long-range utilization of these groups in the *senior leadership development process* of the organization.

At the same time, White males are able to ignore or avoid involvement in and accountability for the affirmative action issues which are produced by the lack of integral involvement of women and minorities in broader aspects of the organization. For most White males in this phase, managing affirmative action is not viewed as a legitimate area for assessing managerial potential or demonstrating managerial competence. Affirmative action is isolated from the mainstream business activities of the organization. It is not a key consideration in organization-wide, long-range planning. Since the organization does not evaluate managers on the basis of their performance on affirmative action related issues, most White males do not identify any personal self-interest in the affirmative action area. Therefore, for most White male managers, affirmative action is a discretionary, extracurricular activity.

This is not true, however, for women or minorities. In addition to their personal concern for the issues that fall within the affirmative action area, there is a general organizational expectation that Black managers and women managers will serve as "experts" on affirmative action. Other minority members are also expected to be the resident expert resource on the culture, feelings and beliefs of their particular group.

As a part of this role, minorities are expected to educate others on the issues, to provide a ready source of information, to serve as a pipeline to others and, in some severe confrontational situations, as conflict mediators. However, although these activities take time and energy away from other duties, the assistance that women and minorities provide in this area is not viewed as an additional role responsibility. While the situation creates extra roles for women and minorities that most White male managers do not possess, these roles are not included in the official performance evaluation and compensation structure of the organization. Minorities and women are, therefore, expected to do these functions in addition to their regular work and still compete with their White male counterparts, who are not burdened with this extra role responsibility. The lack of organizational legitimacy of affirmative action issues produces a whole series of performance and promotion difficulties.

---

[31] In a paper entitled "Well, That All Depends on What the Definition of Is, Is," the author lays out this meaning manipulation process as a distinct strategy used by the power elite to maintain their power.

[32] Please note that this was not called "the President's Committee for ***special or preferential treatment*** of Black people."

[33] Cose, p.132.

— Chapter Four —

SECOND GENERATION AFFIRMATIVE ACTION: A BRIDGE BETWEEN THE GENERATIONS

During the progressive cultural development of a diverse organization, there comes a time when it crosses over from the First Generation to the Second Generation. While there is no clearcut line of demarcation between the two generations, our experience points to one variable that seems to be an essential factor in the evolutionary progression. That variable is *"critical mass."*

Critical mass is not a new concept. It exists, from an organizational perspective, whenever there is a sufficient number of a specific subgroup to begin to significantly impact the character and direction of an organization. However, within the context of the "ending the game" thesis of this book, we will suggest a perspective for the critical mass issue that is new and that may seem revolutionary to some. We have learned in our work both internally and externally with organizations that, under certain conditions and within the structure of a planned organizational change process, the existence of critical mass can be used to initiate a very productive developmental phenomenon.

We cannot define for any organization the magic number of talented Black employees that would be necessary to trigger what we now refer to as the "critical mass phenomenon." We do know, however, that the organization must have enough members to get beyond the "token syndrome" that is characteristic of the issues existing in the First Generation of affirmative action. As we have said, there must be enough diversification to begin to have an impact on the culture of the organization. During the First Generation, there simply is not enough minority group diversity in the organization for anyone to take the needs of these groups seriously or to be concerned about the specific issues that affect them.

It is crucial to understand one important theme that runs throughout the discussions in the text of this book. The cultural change process inherent in managing diversity is a dynamic process. As such, there are two components. First, there are the static parts or elements that must exist in order to place an organization in position to achieve a *multicultural reality*. Second, the existence of a dynamic, systematic, programmatic, integrated set of processes that need to be developing in order to weld the static elements into an active, productive force. The issue of critical mass is no different. It first must exist as an element, and then there must be established processes that activate it as a phenomenon for organizational change.

The "critical mass phenomenon," that is, the active use of interest-group power to achieve a specified objective is nothing new to the capitalistic tradition in America. Throughout our history, the phenomenon has been used by politicians, CEOs, union leaders, ministers, etc. to create legitimacy and momentum for a host of productive causes. What is relatively new, however, is the idea of a creative, proactive and planned use of *critical mass* to move organizations toward the goal of *multiculturalism* in the face of threats from global competition.

If we were able to view critical mass in this way, we would begin to understand that a deeper knowledge of the concept of critical mass significantly reduces the amount of fear of change. We would begin to understand that the person who was brought into the organization by virtue of affirmative action, or based upon the insistence of law, or anything else, came with more than just a Hispanic face or a Black face or a female body. They came with a culture, experience and a perception that contained within it the power to positively impact what the organization is attempting to do. In our experience, critical mass, as we have described it, is necessary throughout the organization's hierarchy in order to ensure that women and minorities have access to the same *informal benefits* which exist for White males in the organization. The phenomenon of *critical mass*, properly managed, helps provide the following benefits:

1. *Critical mass* allows for a sufficient base of support. There are people who can identify with your problems, who understand and are empathetic with the issues you experience.

2. Through *critical mass* a variety of role models and achievement patterns are created so that junior employees can choose career paths that best fit their needs and skills. This is in place of the *one experience fits all* philosophy that can often occur when only a few Black people have "made it."

3. *Critical mass* helps provide an adequate articulation of affirmative action issues. Affirmative action is a complex concept that has, unfortunately, evolved to mean "*the unfair and undeserved acquisition of benefits by minorities.*" We cannot hope to do much to alter this perception in a short book. What we wish to do here is to highlight the fact that critical mass is a factor that allows a smaller or non-dominant group to reach a place where some of its legitimate organizational concerns are seriously considered.

4. *Critical mass* is necessary to ensure individualization. This is an extremely important point. We all know how important individualism is to members of the American culture. Having enough women and minorities throughout the hierarchy of the organization highlights both distinctive individual performance, and the lack of it. Therefore, it helps reduce the tendency to make race or gender the most dominant factor in work relationships.

5. *Critical mass* is an engine that spurs competition. When it is present, it provides White males a variety of people with whom to compete. It is very similar to the impact that Mr. Tiger Woods is currently having on the sport of professional golf. Good, diverse, competition helps to raise the bar rather than lower it.

Instead of being afraid of *critical mass* or just focusing on its individual micro benefits, our experience with *critical mass* suggests that there are many benefits to the organization in general. These benefits will be sorely needed for the challenges of the 21st century and beyond. Some examples are as follows:

1. *Critical mass* manipulation provides needed experience in planned cultural change.

2. *Critical mass* highlights the cultural shortfalls of a system which may need to be fixed, generalized, and systematized. For example, we have found that focusing upon specific issues, like the need for mechanical training or mentoring networks for women or minorities, often revealed a lack of total system mechanisms for ensuring the development of needed skills for all employees.

3. *Critical mass* utilization has a role-modeling effect at both the individual and organizational levels. We have

already mentioned some of the modeling benefits for the individual. At the organizational level, critical mass manipulation allows organizations to learn how to improve. A focus on *critical mass* development increases the talent pool from which the organization may select leaders for higher levels. As more organizations use and implement the benefits of *critical mass*, they become models for others. These resources or people can be used to enter or customize unique markets.

4. *Critical mass* is associated with the "Degrees of Me" concept which is discussed as one of the barriers in Chapter Six. The important issue here is that *critical mass* allows for an expanded definition of "me." In a truly multicultural, global economy, the "me" looks different. Thus, experience with the effective use of *critical mass* will also assist organizations with global marketing strategies.

5. Finally, acceptance of the *critical mass* concept and its benefits allow us to move to a new level. At this level, the organization has the opportunity to build relationships between *critical mass* groups and to bridge them together. Such bridging creates the potential for the organization to gain the benefits of group synergy at the macro or international level of operation.

While the concept of *critical mass*, as we have said, is not new, it is new to begin to focus upon it as an engine for organizational change in the diversity arena. Organizations that have evolved or progressed to the point where they enter the Second Generation of Affirmative Action have the opportunity to realize the value of *critical mass*. Second Generation organizations have the opportunity, through the use of this phenomenon, to consider the numbers of women and minorities needed at each level of the organization to produce the desired benefits and learning. Again, this is an evolutionary process. There is no "quick fix" (Kilmann, 1989). We must have an understanding of the evolutionary process and the issues we are likely to face as we proceed along the way.

We have already indicated that the boundary lines that mark an organization's progression from First Generation Affirmative Action to Second Generation are fuzzy. However, this does not mean that there are no patterns of activity or behavior that allow us to make reasonably good judgments. For example, when an organization moves from the First Generation of Affirmative Action to the Second Generation, it has usually been successful in meeting certain numerical goals with regard to the hiring of women and minorities. Additionally, such organizations have begun to move away from a focus on governmental compliance to a focus on making more use of the heterogeneity that now exists in the organization.

This shift of focus does not mean that all of the first generation issues have been resolved or all the associated problems solved. In fact, many of these issues and problems still remain. However, they have evolved into a subtler, more complex form. In addition, other issues, while essentially resolved, have begun to give rise to new issues and new challenges. Figure 1 in Chapter Two shows the complete list of Second Generation issues treated by Merenivitch and Reigle. We shall continue to limit our discussion to those points that are more relevant to the objectives that are the foundation of this book.

Second Generation Affirmative Action Issues

(1) A Sense that "Racism and Sexism are Dead": Second Generation issues are usually experienced after an organization has been successful in achieving *critical mass* as defined and discussed in the first part of this Chapter.

While there is potential for many benefits, the situation initially produces frustration for many members of the organization. Organizations that reach the Second Generation of Affirmative Action experience themselves as having already invested a tremendous amount of time and resources, in good faith, to bring Black people, women and other minority groups on board.

A prevalent assumption made by much of the White leadership and White membership of the organization is that their successes in this area demonstrate that *"racism and sexism"* are dead and have been given a proper burial. The belief is that most of the big problems have been solved and, for many of those who take this view, the organization is now *"beyond all that."* Such attitudes, unfortunately, often lead to increased complacency and inaction. Herein lies the basis for the impending frustration.

The reality of the situation is that both individual and institutional expressions of racism and sexism have not disappeared but, rather, have been transformed into less overt and less hostile forms. We can understand some of the character of this shift by relating it to the natural difference in the responses of people to negative elements that are viewed from an "outside" versus an "inside" perspective. Let's use the family as a metaphor.

Prior to the creation of *critical mass,* most women and minority groups were clearly perceived as "outside" the family of the organization. Consequently, they receive the harsh, overt and often hostile criticism usually reserved for outsiders. Once enough minority group members are brought inside the organization and establish an "inside identity," the criticism becomes less overt and hostile. The important point, however, is to remain aware that many of the former feelings, attitudes, as well as the anxiety associated with them, are still present. They are likely to be denied when openly challenged but can be observed in other forms.

Some of the negative attitudes show up as "residual stereotypes." Due to increased interaction between Black people and White people, White male employees begin to move away from an almost total inability to see valuable aspects of Black employees. The difficulty in perceiving value is part of the "deficit model" which will be discussed more fully in Chapter Six. As time goes on, White people become better able to perceive a range of behavior from women and minorities rather than lumping them all into one group. But the stereotypes and negative assumptions still remain in subtle forms. An example of the subtlety is that whites will *doubt whether most minorities and women can succeed* rather than *expect them to fail*.

In the First Generation, the way an organization dealt with racial issues became a model for managing gender issues, or vice versa. In the Second Generation, *dividing the pie* becomes an issue where the victims of *racism* and *sexism* are pitted against each other. Instead of integrating the generic aspects of *racism* and *sexism* and addressing their systemic components, the questions become dichotomous. How much effort and resources should be devoted to solving racism issues, and how much to solving sexism issues? Another issue is a concern over whether *Affirmative Action* progress has become unbalanced in favor of minorities or women?

Even though race and gender are pitted against one another in the Second Generation, these issues begin to have a legitimate place in boss-subordinate and other business discussions. Managers begin to recognize that race and sex are potentially contributing factors in performance and interpersonal problems and that they are, therefore, legitimate topics for investigation and discussion. The problem is that employees show differing skill levels and comfort levels as they work in these areas. The main responsibility for opening such discussion still rests primarily with the women and *minorities*. So, what seems on the surface to be okay is not really okay.

(2) Career Disillusionment: Another area of confusion and frustration during the Second Generation occurs in the arena of career progression. Black people begin to feel increasing uncertainty and pessimism about the potential for their careers. At each level they find they have to deal with the same pressures to *"prove themselves"* that they faced at the previous levels. The insidious aspect of this *"prove yourself phenomenon"* is that White male employees experience the *prove yourself* pressure also. However, for Black employees and Women, the prove yourself challenge is juxtaposed against an accompanying doubt in their ability to succeed. This tends to become evidence to Black people and women that successes that are realized in one position are not readily accepted as demonstrations of acquired competence or preparation for a higher position. In other words, there seems to be little carry forward of success accomplished at a lower level. Instead, successful performance for individuals from these groups are frequently experienced as "exceptions" or "surprises" which, then, requires additional performance success to refute.[34]

Even when the success of women and Black people is not treated as a surprise, they experience less power related to their roles than that which is available to their White male counterparts. In addition to the power that is derived from one's hierarchical position, a person's power also depends upon his or her involvement with and access to a number of informal organizational network systems. White employees simply have more access to and "perceived fit" within such networks. Consequently, White male and female employees often are able to rise more easily to top levels while Black employees experience more blocks to their advancement. As the disillusionment of minorities with career opportunities within the organization becomes evident, they are viewed as less motivated and less loyal. In the most unfortunate cases, Black people who complain may be labeled with the "not a team player" tag with the associated negative result that their advancement becomes further delayed or even threatened.

(3) Implementing Accountability: In the Second Generation phase of an organization's development toward *multiculturalism,* the accountability question comes into focus. It becomes clear that *Affirmative Action* and the management of a diverse work force need to be "part of the job" and not an extracurricular activity for managers. It is generally recognized that many White managers lack ability to manage minorities and women well. We make a clear distinction here between the "ability to manage" and the "ability to control."

This inability to manage can be viewed as a level of managerial incompetence rather than a failure on the part of *minorities* and women to adapt to the organization. The issue now is how to ensure that inability or unwillingness to function effectively in a multicultural environment has correspondingly negative career implications as the inability to manage any other significant part of the business. Thinking and discussion begins on how to ensure that *multicultural management* joins other areas of the business as a legitimate area for demonstrating managerial competence and career potential.

(4) Constituency Development: The dual role of minorities and women, which surfaces in the First Generation, is now recognized; but as *minorities* and women reach managerial levels, their burden increases rather than disappears. This is a phenomenon that has been referred to as "the minority tax." It represents the extra responsibilities that women and minorities are often expected to, or feel obligated to, perform. It is simply not possible for a woman manager to steer clear of woman/man issues or for a Black manager to avoid involvement in Minority/White issues. Black and female managers must constantly determine the level of their involvement in these issues — both within and outside their immediate work area. For example, they may need to decide whether to join a task force on *Affirmative Action* or how to respond when requested to assist a woman or *minority-group member* in another part of the organization. Avoiding such situations is next to impossible when the person is one of the "successful few" in a First Generation Organization, but becomes a matter of strategic choice in the Second Generation where more successful examples exist. In all of this, however, there is a justifiable concerned with how (or whether) the people providing this assistance will be rewarded or compensated for their contributions in the area of *Affirmative Action.*

The development of the Second Generation also brings a new focus to the "white backlash" concerns of the First Generation. As people experience changes in the organizational makeup, White males perceive threats to their own effectiveness and to their career opportunities. Some feel that certain *Affirmative Action Programs* give women and/or *minorities* an "unfair advantage." The organization becomes sensitive to actual and potential accusations of *reverse discrimination.* Thus, White males simply become one of the specific cultural interest groups whose needs must be considered in the context of the entire multicultural fabric of the organization. In other words, they become one of the cultural groups that sit at the multicultural table rather than the entire table around which all other groups must fit.

(5) Affirmative Action and Organizational Development: Whether an organization realizes the situation or not, the issues of the Second Generation of Affirmative Action bring with them more positive opportunities than the frustrations and difficult challenges we have discussed thus far. The issues of the Second Generation also create a kind of energy that offers a tremendous opportunity for greater organizational development. We covered some of this potential in our discussion of the benefits of *critical mass*. Rather than being thought of as a separate and distinct area of concern, the issues of the *Second Generation of Affirmative Action* could be recognized as a stimulant for planned organizational change, the kind of change that goes beyond increasing the membership and participation of Black people and other "minorities."

We have argued that building an *effective multicultural organization* is, in reality, a cultural change process moving through the resolution of First and Second Generation Affirmative Action Issues. An organization that has successfully implemented *Affirmative Action Programs* finds itself in a much better position to deal with change of any sort. The accumulated learning and developed skills are adaptable to other issues, such as union-management relationships, selection and development of managers for both domestic and international assignments, and the challenges for older employees.

Efforts to resolve concerns created through *Affirmative Action* also help improve an organization's *benefit infrastructure.* For example, a program whose initial thrust was to deal with the problems relating to career and skill development programs, performance appraisal and feedback, communications, and decision making for *minorities*, often results in system changes which produce beneficial change for White males as well.

Accepting the challenges of the Second Generation also hold benefits that help improve the performance of White males in their managerial roles. White males in management have many questions regarding their role in the *Affirmative Action* activities of the Second Generation. For example: How do I become a leader in Affirmative Action? How do I deal with the pressures from my own peers when I become proactive in Affirmative Action? Will I really be evaluated on the basis of how well I deal with minorities as well as how I carry out other responsibilities? How will success or failure in this area affect my future? Addressing such questions as those listed above requires the kind of flexibility of thought that surrounds most situations of innovation and change. The ability to be "flexible" in one's thinking, point of view or paradigm is a key ingredient both for innovation and for directing and monitoring the kinds of incremental changes that are part of cultural change processes.[35]

[34] See "Pluralism and Performance" in Chapter Six.

[35] Some examples of success in this area can be reviewed in the book, *Beyond Race and Gender: Unleashing the Power of Your Total Workforce by Managing Diversity,* by Dr. Roosevelt Thomas.

— Chapter Five —

NURTURING: THE PLANNED CHANGE PROCESS

An organization that *has* reached the Second Generation of Affirmative Action has a diverse work force. That is, its employees differ significantly in race, gender and ethnic background. Most organizations today have or soon will have diverse work forces. It is no longer feasible, acceptable, or economically productive to start up or perpetuate a large organization with an all-White/all-male work force and culture.

Since, for many organizations, the *diversity* of its work force has been achieved by the "adding on" versus the "starting up with" method, a lot of effort and focused planned changes need to take place to "nurture" the organizational system from one type of culture to another. The normal tendency upon hearing the concept of nurture is to think about individuals, as in a parent's role with small children. However, we are using the term with reference to an entire unit, department or organizational system.

We use the term "nurture" to emphasize the care, sensitivity, respect and communication that will be required. If an organization did not begin with an integrated, diverse work force, it will require concerned *nurturing* as it moves through the cultural change necessary to become a fully *multicultural system*. Most organizations in the last half of the 20th Century came to realize this essential fact, hence there was a tremendous proliferation of programs, lectures, workshops, books and articles on the pros and cons of "managing work force diversity." The nurturing concept helps us to focus on the actual objective of all this work.

An organization that operates effectively in utilizing its diverse work force can be described as a *multicultural organization.* The key phrase here is "effective in utilizing." A diverse work force does not in itself constitute a *multicultural organization. Multiculturalism* implies an active integration of the cultural diversity existing within the organization. Effective integration will not occur by osmosis. In other words, the mere affirmation of the desire for diversity, or even the apparent success in obtaining diverse representation, is insufficient to achieve the result of *multiculturalism.*

Merenivitch and Reigle, in their discussion of the "Principles for Design and Development of Multicultural Organizations," outlined the organizational criteria which are necessary for a truly *multicultural organization* (1979, p.8). Their criteria are listed below:

- It actively seeks to capitalize on the advantages of its diversity — rather than attempting to stifle or ignore the diversity — and to minimize the barriers that can develop as a result of people's having different backgrounds, attitudes, values, behavior styles and concerns.

- Organizational resources (key jobs, income, prerequisites, access to information, etc.) are distributed equitably and are not determined or affected by cultural characteristics such as race or gender.

- The ability to influence decisions and the way they are carried out is shared widely, not differentially by cultural characteristics.

- The organizational culture (assumptions about people and groups, the take-it-for-granted norms, the way work gets done) is pluralistic in that it recognizes and appreciates diversity. It acknowledges both the need for "being the same" in some ways to work together effectively and the need for "being different" in some ways to recognize and tap into individual and group interests, concerns, and backgrounds.

- Institutional policies, practices, and procedures are flexible and responsive to the needs of all employees.

We decided to quote from Merenivitch and Reigle for several reasons. First, it is an excellent characterization of the kinds of activities and capacities that would be exhibited by a *multicultural organization*. Second, since this work was published in 1979, it reveals an extraordinary amount of vision. Finally, and perhaps most importantly, the authors indicate that these elements or characteristics are brought about through the use of "principles" which are concepts or processes that reflect a systematic, holistic character.[36]

Multicultural status, as typified in an ideal sense within the characteristics stated above, is the goal toward which organizations ought to be striving as they move through the First and Second Generations of Affirmative Action. The task is much larger than periodic "head counts" to make sure we are in compliance with arbitrary minimum standards. The task is even larger than attempting to soothe our collective moral conscience by "doing the right thing." In truth, it is a matter of "capital investment," of doing everything we can to receive the greatest return on our invested "human capital."

Business executives don't seem to have any difficulty understanding the value of diversification with regard to financial portfolios or an organization's product line. However, many suddenly develop a kind of intellectual incapacity or what we like to refer to as "learned ignorance" when it comes to seeing the value of diversity in the human system. *Nurturing* an organization through the complex social changes on the way to *multiculturalism* requires more than acquiring and applying a range of techniques that have been developed within the disciplines of organizational development, psychology, anthropology, or management. *Nurturing* is a complex process which requires a set of guiding principles. Constructing a truly *multicultural organization* is achieved by applying these guiding principles.

Before we discuss the principles, it is important to convey the proper philosophical perspective. A successful process for *managing diversity* in organizations needs to begin with a "dynamic, systematic, holistic paradigm." This is why we present our examination of the key items involved in the form of *principles*. This formulation is not a loose, sloppy or "cute" way to use some very familiar terms. It is a serious recognition of both the vital importance of the elements being examined and of the complexity in the number of paths that might be taken to secure them. Whatever path is taken in a particular diversity program, there must be a recognition of the importance of the following "principles" to secure the quality of the end product.

(1) The Principle of Heterogeneity.

Research from many fields spanning a number of years has documented the value of heterogeneity (i.e. diversity). This has been exhibited in the form of such things as "alloys in metals," "synthetic blends in fabrics," "mutual fund portfolios in finance," "brainstorming in problem solving," etc. It has also been brought into practical use within the intellectual and business communities in the form of the "think tanks" and "skunk works." Because of all this work and the years of solid research which has supported the value of heterogeneity in a variety of forms, we believe we can make one categorical statement — "Diversity is valuable and we already know it is valuable." Diversity brings strength, the potential for a clarity of ideas, creativity and a variety of approaches to a problem as well as different methods for implementing solutions.

However, we must be clear about another fact implicit in all of the research. Diverse elements brought together and then left in the isolation of their own uniqueness will not produce any of the benefits which the research has shown. The true value of heterogeneity stems from the "proactive processes" that are used to integrate the different elements into a new and better composite product. Heterogeneity standing alone is just a static concept that reflects one of the elements of the mix. The "principle of heterogeneity," however, focuses upon the necessity for a process that will integrate the different elements into a new and better whole.

We live in a *culturally pluralistic society*. The organizations in existence and the employees within them are products of that society. All groups making up the organization need to be seen as integral parts of the system rather than "extra parts that have been added on by compliance or convenience." If we are to receive any of the benefits which the research documents, diversity must be recognized and managed rather than glorified or ignored.

To *manage diversity* means that we must establish external and internal processes that are aimed at integrating the diverse reservoirs of human resources into the core processes of the business. It is essential that human diversity begin to be viewed as providing opportunities to be utilized rather than headaches to be tolerated or avoided. Identifying and establishing such processes will not be easy. They never are. The key barriers outlined in Chapter Six help us to begin to focus on some of the fundamental impediments standing in the way of significant progress toward integrating the diversity inherent in people of color.

(2) The Principle of People as Individuals and as Group Members.

The American culture is one that idolizes its creed of individual effort, individual initiative, individual accomplishments, etc. (Lipset, 1992). The sanctity of the individual has allowed this country to foster and support "up from bootstraps innovation" within the context of an organized society. The idea of individual rights is firmly established and the Constitution protects the individual from the greater power of the state or collective.

Protections for individual rights are so strong that sometimes they operate to the detriment of society's sense of justice or the community good. But, however strong the belief in and commitment to the value of individualism, (what the individual can do) the truth of the matter is that very little can be accomplished or sustained by the "organization of one." The individual and the group are inextricably linked in the process of human development. Even with the focus on individualism in our culture, there is a strong sense of group identification and group membership. People will readily identify themselves as part of many groups and will alter their behavior with reference to the norms from these groups: CEOs, unions, Blacks, Whites, Italians, Irish, Jewish, Southerners, Northerners, Californians, preppies, nerds, underclass, homeless, the press, academics, et al. Group identification helps us simplify our lives by facilitating our interaction with people. However, group focus also allows us to gloss over or ignore individuality. In either event, to deny the potent impact of group membership and group identification in our society is to deny simple reality.

Every person is an individual. Each of us possesses a unique set of strengths, weaknesses, and needs. To deal with each other on the basis of accurate information, we must be able to perceive others in the work force as unique people apart from particular reference to their group homogeneity as characterized by race, gender, or other classifications. This is necessary to help us avoid making sweeping generalizations and assumptions about the abilities and personality traits of other people and it provides us the opportunity to take advantage of the special skills and abilities of each person.

At the same time that we recognize the uniqueness of the individual, we also know that the racial, ethnic, gender, and other groupings to which individuals belong affect their experiences, the nature of other people's expectations of them, the way they are treated, the social pressures on them, and their job performance. Therefore, in order to take advantage of the resources of diversity, we must be willing, not only to view individuals as unique contributors but also to recognize the effects of cultural background on their work effectiveness. The "Principle of People as Individuals and as Group Members" offers the perspective that helps us remember and capitalize on this twofold reality. Groups are important elements of support for the individual. An understanding of this principle will assist the organization in building its capability by capitalizing upon and utilizing the natural support offered by the different groupings within the workplace.

Organizational groups (such as Black Managers' Workteam, Women Managers' Core Group, or White Managers' Taskforces) provide opportunities for individuals to share experiences, identify norms and patterns, develop skills for dealing with different situations, and to re-examine areas that may need to be changed. These groups may be helpful in enabling the organization to devise and develop better integrative mechanism and, as a result, higher quality production.

The divisions listed above were unique to our experience in the Procter & Gamble Paper Products Plant located in Albany, Georgia. (The story of this plant is highlighted in the book *Rising Tide* by Davis Dyer, Frederick Dalzell and Rowena Olegario, pp. 166-175.) The plant stands not only as a shining example of diversity management, but its 30-plus years of superior performance support the principle of economic diversity that we propose.

(3) The Principle of Shared Responsibility.

Whether recognized or acknowledged, the reality of any social system is that the quantity and quality of its output is a function of the actions and interactions of everyone who is a part of the system. Maintaining the effectiveness of the *multicultural organization* is a responsibility shared by everyone in the organization. All employees must be actively involved in a continuing review and refinement of organizational norms, climate, practices, and patterns of behavior so that they will be supportive of the goals of a *multicultural organization*.

In the area of *diversity management*, this means that White males and White females must be proactive in racial matters, not relying solely on minority men and women to define issues and problem areas. However, to be able to put forth their creative effort in this area, White men and women cannot continue to be made to feel as if the fault for all minority problems rests at their doorstep. The release of White people from the dysfunction of this blaming process is part of the Black employee's responsibility and part of their contribution to the progress toward a multicultural organization.

The *Principle of Shared Responsibility* requires the organization to formally recognize and declare that no groups will be victimized or left out. It also requires that the organization establish procedures that will ensure this result. Finally, the principle requires a fundamental recognition that what happens in the organization is everyone's responsibility. The entire organization will be strengthened by addressing the needs of individuals and subgroups and by the insistence of different groups on higher quality contribution to the organization by their members.

(4) The Principle of Deliberate, Continuous, Planned Change.

Building an effective *multicultural organization* is an effort that must be planned and managed. It must be managed in much the same manner as any other major aspect of the business. It will not "just happen" without management attention and resources. Aspects of this principle include the following items taken from the report by Merenivitch and Reigle (1979):

(a) A new production module or department, progressing through start-up to normal operations, does not do so in "one great leap," but in a series of smaller steps. Similarly, an organization cannot move from all-White/all male work force to diverse work force to multicultural organization in one jump. Instead, there will be separate phases in the development process, each of which must be analyzed, planned, and managed in order to move on successfully to the next phase.

(b) Just as equipment requires periodic preventive maintenance, a multicultural organization requires periodic reviews involving the entire social system and its progress in becoming multicultural. Such maintenance is necessary to keep the system on track toward its goals, to continually refine objectives, and to keep goal-directed energy at a level sufficient to produce results.

(c) The information needed to accomplish (a) and (b) above must be complete and accurate in order to measure progress and identify needs for corrective action. This requires that methods and systems be designed and used to collect and analyze information about the functioning of the organization.

(d) Commitment of resources (time, money, and people) must accompany the planning of the changes. Without resources, the work needed to move the organization ahead will not get done. Further, people often "read" the level of importance accorded a project by the type and level of resources devoted to it.

(5) The Principle of Self-Interest.

Most human motivation can be characterized as movement fostered by and in the direction of one's personal interest. Organizations, likewise, as entities built by human beings out of the human experience, move on the energy of self-interest. To get most organizations to move requires that we build a "business case" that shows the benefit of a project, either as a potential positive gain or as the avoidance of a potential negative loss.

The "Principle of Self-Interest" requires us to focus on specific benefits. If we combine this principle with the previous one concerning *deliberate, continuous, planned change,* it suggests that we must actively search for the benefits or opportunities in organizations rather than waiting for them to be shown to us. A recent quotation from one minister's sermon captured it this way "If you can't see it before you see it, then you won't see it."

It is the organization's responsibility to define how being multicultural helps it to achieve its business and quality-of-work-life objectives and goals. In other words, a primary function of leadership is to construct the frame of reference that will enable employees to understand how and why the movement toward *multiculturalism* is important to the organization and to help people identify with their individual role and responsibility in making it happen. Why do we say this?

Let's return a moment to the first paragraph of this section. In that paragraph we said that individual motivation is fostered by self-interest. We continued on to say that "organizations, likewise, as entities built by human beings out of the human experience, move on the energy of self-interest." Now on the surface, one might think we were attempting to endow the organization, which we know is not alive, with living human qualities. Obviously, we are not seriously attempting to do this. The real question in our minds is, "Who is it within an organization that has the direct responsibility for articulating and securing its self-interest." It doesn't take much thought to realize that this responsibility, whether accepted or not, whether executed well or poorly, clearly belongs in the hands of the organization's leadership.

While it may seem like an unnecessary diversion, we believe it is important at this particular time to say a few words about *leaders* and the *function of leadership* in organizations.[37] Leadership commitment is one of the complex list of interactive barriers that hampers and often prevents organizations from progressively developing through the Stages of Affirmative Action to Multiculturalism. It is clear to us that without someone in a leadership position stepping forward and exercising the true *function of leadership*, very little can be done to rid our organizations of these pervasive barriers. Therefore, we must raise a few questions. What is *leadership*? Who are *leaders* and how would we know one if we saw one? What is the true *function of leadership*? Are there any real answers to such "heady" questions?

During the latter part of the twentieth century, in both the popular and research literature, there was a good deal of interest in determining whether there is a real difference between "leadership" and "management." Stated a different way, is a "leader" different from a "manager" and, if so, how? First of all, we need to say that the activity of leadership is a continuum, an evolutionary process and not a static "cause and effect" set of steps arranged in some action sequence. The person who is a leader does distinct things, this is true, but those things are done in recognition of the process, that is, the fact that his or her actions are being applied to a moving continuum of interactive events.

A leader recognizes the fact that most adults, and perhaps most human beings, learn through the process of discovery. With this recognition, the true leader is a person who creates the conditions which will be conducive to "adult discovery learning." In essence, the leader creates the conditions for people to experiment, explore, contribute and even to fail without the fear of failure. The good leader does this through clarity of vision, real or practical analysis of the *current reality* and the identification and creation of processes that enable people to begin to visualize a path for getting to the vision.

The leader is confronted, first, with the record of past experiences and accomplishments; second, with the uncertainty of the present challenge; and, finally, he or she is faced with the reality of the relentless pace of time. Whatever the leader decides, the fact remains that he or she, along with time will "move on." At such points, the leader is the person who chooses to lead. What does this mean?

In the face of a new challenge in the *current reality*, the leader chooses his or her *vision*, crystallizes the vision, and then communicates it. This, in essence, is the *function of leadership*. The difference between the leader's vision and the *current reality* creates what we refer to as "structural tensions." These tensions emerge as a result of the gap that exists between the leader's conceptual ideal (vision) and the socio-cultural reality (how things are now). The tensions arise out of the anxieties that are created as a function of uncertainty and dissonance about how we will get there or whether we will get there. As with all social situations, someone benefits from the way things currently are; therefore, anyone suggesting a different approach is rattling the "comfort cage." The leader's job is to create the vision which often produces this unsettling situation, and then guide the system to a new position of comfort.

If this is what leaders do, then there must be a different set of choices and actions for those who operate as managers. A manager doesn't view his or her role as one of creating new visions. Managers view their job as dealing mainly with *current reality* and establishing coping strategies that allow the organization to survive the challenges created by changing conditions within the *current reality* of the organization.

Obviously, from such a frame of reference, we do not define leadership as a function of a hierarchical position. It helps to have organizational clout but that clout can be used either to support the *function of leadership*, to *manage* or, as a third option, to not exercise it at all as in the case of someone who wishes to be a person who follows. Although both leaders and managers are necessary for the system's progress, it is the "function of true leadership" that is most important to the reconciliation of the issues arising from the need for *diversity management*.

(6) The Principle of Accountability.

Accountability is the gyroscopic mechanism that helps keep the people and the system on course. If the course is deemed to be an error, the *Principle of Deliberate, Continuous Planned Change* can operate to alter it. Accountability is necessary for any objective that we seriously hope to achieve. This concept reflects the need to examine and evaluate all outcomes against objectives. Effort and intent are good but they are not excuses for the failure to achieve reasonable objectives. There is always the need for the "teeth" of accountability in the management process of planned change. Leaders in a multi-cultural organization must be held accountable for its vision or the lack of it.

Accountability is being responsible for achieving results, for making things happen. Managers in a *multicultural organization* must be held accountable for initiating, directing, and controlling the processes that help to make individuals and groups effective in achieving multicultural goals and objectives. Other members of the organization must be accountable as well. To build and support a multicultural organization, every employee must be accountable for:

(a) understanding the nature of multicultural organizations.

(b) contributing to the implementation, effectiveness and maintenance of the organization as a multicultural system.

(c) adjusting their personal behaviors and skills to meet the requirements of working effectively in a multicultural environment.

The proper perspective for operating in a multicultural organization must be an "us" view of the system. The "we/they" perspective so prevalent in the first and Second Generations must be gradually transformed into a system of different cultural groups but all with a sense of common interests.

---

[36] It is vital to understand that "principle-based management" is the way to achieve what we are calling "multiculturalism. Non-integrated diversity programs, techniques, workshops, etc., while very useful in some ways, will not get you there.

[37] As an additional resource, we suggest the re-reading of the classic book by Chester Bernard, *The Function of the Executive.*

— Chapter Six —

KEY BARRIERS TO THE PROGRESSION OF A FUNCTIONING MULTICULTURAL ORGANIZATION

Anyone who has ever been involved in significant organizational change is aware that it is easy to identify elements that we desire to have in place and things that we might want to be changed to move forward. However, it is quite another matter to effectively implement new ideas (Rogers, 1992). Changing from a First Generation Affirmative Action organization to a diverse *multicultural entity* is very difficult. Putting aside the issue which frequently comes up with regard to whether people want to make changes consistent with any *affirmative action* agenda, organizational change is an extremely difficult process.

It is particularly difficult when, as in the case of *diversity management*, the major focus of the change is the organization's own "cherished" *culture*. A medical analogy may assist us here in making our point. The *critical mass phenomenon* that we have said is associated with effective *multicultural* development, when it is large enough, begins to threaten or shake the fundamental roots of the organization's established *culture*. This activates a type of "cultural defense system" similar in concept and effect to the antibody defense system within the human body.

We will refer to these protectors of the current organizational system as "cultural interferons." Their purpose is to protect the organization from any "foreign bodies" unless the intruders can be proved to be benign. The organization was designed and evolved with its *culture*; it became effective or successful with its *culture*; it is comfortable and familiar with its way of doing things. Now, something or someone comes along to tell it that it must change. What intelligent person wouldn't expect serious resistance?

It is within the context of the imagery created above that we will examine some of the key barriers that exist to the development of an effective *multicultural organization*. We do not purport to have isolated all of the barriers that are operational within organizations striving to become truly *multicultural*. However, as with the other sections of this book, we have critically reviewed our experience in this area and identified what we believe to be the most difficult and elusive of the barriers we have encountered in that experience. We believe that any organizational leader seriously interested in his or her organization becoming *multicultural* should meditate on these barriers and the action implications associated with them.

One important point before we begin. While we will discuss these barriers one by one, they are inescapably intertwined. One barrier may, for example, affect and strengthen the negative impact of another. This is true of the barriers of *Floating Criteria* and *Degrees of Me*. In order to maintain the perceived effectiveness and comfort of the *Degrees of Me*, White people in power will maintain almost a death grip on their prerogative to utilize Floating Criteria in selecting those who receive the most important organizational positions. The barriers we discuss in this chapter are the key elements, which have evolved over time and stand in place to maintain the *status quo* of the dominant *Eurocentric culture* of American corporate life.

Barrier One: The Lack of Top Leadership Commitment

Can anything happen in an organization without top management support? The answer is yes! Yet, our position is that it is impossible for major, systematic, planned organization change to take place without commitment from the top. *Managing diversity* effectively requires major, systematic, planned organizational change. Therefore, in organizations which are *managing diversity* well, you will find true commitment from management at the very top of the organization. What do we mean by "true" commitment?

The answer to this question is not as difficult or fuzzy as it may first appear. However, it will require an ability to "translate," or better yet, to "trans-relate." For example, suppose an organization that is positioned in a dying industry was considering a major change process that would move it to an entirely new but thriving industry. No intelligent person would believe that an organization in this position would try to accomplish this without the most intimate involvement and commitment from its top management group. Now, what do we mean by "intimate" involvement? If a company was changing industries in order to survive, we would realize, almost immediately, that it would demand top management involvement, especially in such activities as goal setting, resource assessment and allocation. Top Management would also make themselves available for meetings designed to communicate the new direction, to address concerns and to stress accountability, that is, the processes for "holding people's feet to the fire."

Prior to any communication and/or movement, top management would have made some assessment of the expected impact of the change on the company's profitability. There would also be some type of acknowledgment of a probable initial dip in normal levels of productivity. This is not a process that would be "delegated" to some obscure staff organization or placed into the hands of an outside consulting firm to accomplish for the company. Now, "trans-relate" these activities back to the area of *managing diversity* and the question of top management commitment becomes clearer.

Managing diversity, like changing industries, involves personal and career risks. In such situations most employees of an organization will want to "wait for the signal from the top." If top managers are not involved and committed, they send the clear signal that the project, in spite of what they say about it, is not really important to the life of the business. As with the process of changing industries, the process of *managing diversity* cannot be successfully communicated with the spoken word or with neatly typed memos.

Employees must see "behavior" from top managers consistent with the words and memos. If the logic of this illustration is clear, why doesn't it often transfer into the kind of top management commitment necessary to accomplish the stated objectives of many diversity programs? We believe that part of the answer lies in the *deficit model paradigm* and in a failure to apply the active part of the "principle of self-interest" already discussed in Chapter Five. Top management and key executive have yet to discover a business reason for doing what we believe they have the technology, experience and resources to do. Perhaps the inescapable reality of the demographic changes in American population makeup will provide the necessary business reason. However, with the dawning of the 21st Century and the knowledge of changing demographic data, American companies are still holding to behavior patterns of the past. The prerequisite motivation for change still does not appear to exist at the top levels of corporate management.

Barrier Two: The Deficit Model and the Racism Model

We believe that the most insidious barrier to the full integration of members from *African American Culture* and, maybe, all *minority*[38] cultures, is the existence of and the interplay between two very strong explanatory models or *paradigms*. We call them *The Deficit Model* (Merenivitch & Reigle, 1979; Cobb, 1989; Batts, 1990) and *The Racism Model.*

The Deficit Model is the real and pervasive belief among most White people, and many Black people as well, that Black people are innately deficient. That is, a belief that Black people are inferior to White people on almost any performance criteria we might consider. Many White people feel that anything that is done for Black people will be ineffective because we "really are deficient" in all of the crucial areas needed for human and organizational progress (i.e., intelligence, responsibility, education, ambition, communication skills, behavior, dependability, etc.). According to this model, most of the problems of Black people can be attributed to their inherent inferiority. People subscribing to this model believe, further, that almost all efforts initiated to help Black people will fail so they view such efforts with a good deal of skepticism and some resentment. How does such a model account for Black talent and success?

Business or economic success is usually attributed to *affirmative action* or viewed as some other form of *special treatment*; academic achievement is often explained away as an "exception to the rule." Success may also be assigned to attendance at White schools, if any are in the person's background; athletic and musical success is normally explained by "extra natural ability." It is interesting, but sometimes irritating, to hear sports commentators refer to the play of a basketball star like Larry Bird as the result of "yeomen's work" or "blue collar effort" thus indicating a superior work ethic and then call the play of Michael Jordon or Magic Johnson, "natural ability."

The conclusion of the twentieth century, however, has produced a personal phenomenon that may help to remove forever the fog of the "natural ability deficit model." We could refer to this phenomenon as the "Tiger Woods Factor." He is an example of a unique personality and talent that is simply outside all the boxes. He is a Black man. He is also Asian; therefore, he is distinctly multicultural. He is intelligent and articulate. He attended an elite predominantly White University. At one point in the history of this country, Mr. Woods would not have been permitted to develop or to display his enormous golf skill. If we were still in one of those periods, America would have continued to assert that the golf play of members of the dominant cultural group represented the "best in the entire world." The extraordinary play of Mr. Tiger Woods introduced the "Tiger Woods Factor," which is a simple reminder that without the embracing of true diversity, America may be celebrating performance that it believes is superior when it is really mediocre. Since it has been confronted with the Tiger Woods Factor, the golf world is doing now what we would expect all organizations to do in a truly multicultural environment. The golf world has been forced to raise the bar of its own productivity.

The counterpart to the *Deficit Model* is *The Racism Model*. It is a *paradigm* held by most Black people and some White people. It explains the difficulties experienced by Black people and other *minorities* of color by blaming them on the racist attitudes and discriminatory practices of White people. How does this model account for the positive behavior of those White people who don't seem to possess a racist attitude. Often it discounts these attitudes by relating them to a sense of guilt but, more often, the person holding this model waits for those special pressure situations when "the White person's true colors will be displayed." We believe that virtually every individual raised within the Americ*an Culture* has experience with either *The Deficit Model* or *The Racism Model* and that parts of these explanatory systems are ingrained in their psyche and, maybe, embedded into the marrow of their bones.

The subtle effects of a history of isolation — first slavery, then, segregation, and discrimination — have created a truly ironic situation in the nature of American race relations.

First, it has created the need to do specific things with regard to Black people in order to integrate them into mainstream American life. At the same time, the isolation has prevented a sufficient amount of positive interaction between the races needed to reduce the deep-seated negative and prejudicial beliefs that each group holds with respect to the other.

On the other hand, *The Racism Model*, supported by many Black people, causes us to be skeptical of the motives of all White people. It is almost impossible to believe that they will ever do anything lasting to open the doors of opportunity for us to the American Dream. One insight gleaned from the evolutionary history of race relations in America helps us appreciate the invidiousness, if not the insanity, of *The Deficit and The Racism Models*. As we examine our experience and our memories for data to support that experience, it is true that each of us could point to a tremendous amount of information that might support the accuracy of either model. Dr. William Shockley had spent the better part of a long career amassing evidence to do exactly that with respect to *The Deficit Model*. Some people may feel that Rev. Al Sharpton of New York has been doing a similar thing with respect to *The Racism Model*.

Those of us who don't accept the theory of the inherent inferiority of African Americans find that we still have to remain vigilant in order to maintain our confidence in Black people's capability against a wealth of curious, questionable, empirical phenomena. For example, why do we as a people in post slavery times continue to remain on the bottom rung of American society, a society renowned for its freedom and opportunity? Why is it that, regardless of the progress or rate of progress that we appear to make, we seem to be forever locked into cycles of repetitive civil rights activity every twenty or thirty years? Why is it that, with all of the resources we have been able to acquire, in spite of discriminatory systems, we can't seem to find a way to pool these resources and cooperate together. Cooperation is necessary in order to build the type of organizations and communities that would provide the foundation for Black people to leap frog to the next level of collective achievement (Willis, 1992).

These are not new questions. They have been asked often in the recent and distant past. In fact, the two models being discussed in this section have emerged as major conceptions for explaining these puzzling questions. Most of the proponents of each model are smug in their confidence that their model explains the facts. We have said that White people who are proponents of *The Deficit Model* believe that the existence of these questions proves inherent racial inferiority. The proponents of *The Racism Model*, who are mostly Black people, view the existence of these realities as proof of the bigotry and discrimination still rampant in America.

Given the pervasiveness of the two models and the perspective taken in this book, what are the options? One clear choice is to stay in our individual camps like feudal lords from Medieval history slinging arrows and fireballs blindly over the walls at each other. That activity, however, won't provide either camp with the objective information needed to understand the reality of life behind the walls of our isolated "feudal racial castles." With access to such information we could construct an effective bridge to realistic communication, to new hope.

A second choice is the perspective offered by us in this book. We have chosen to examine the diversity situation in America as a historical phenomenon. With regard to the two specific models being discussed here, one insight has emerged. We now see that the proponents of both models have a serious flaw in their perspective. Both groups have tended to focus more on the articulation and defense of their respective models, constructed to explain reality, than on examining the evolutionary development of reality and determining what can be done "given the facts as they happen to be." Neither the Deficit or Racism models are productive because they embrace the strategy of placing blame on another as their basic objective. One blames the victim and the other blames a "*generic White oppressor.*"

Nancy Friday, in her initial book, *My Mother, Myself,* makes a very important point with respect to the uselessness of such blaming. In the section from which the quotation is taken, Ms. Friday is discussing the resolution of conflict in the symbiotic Mother/Daughter relationship:

> *In the name of fairness, and reality too, let me add an important postscript which is true not only for this chapter but of this whole book. Looking over our shoulder at what mother may or may not have done so many years ago locks us into the past. "She did it. There is nothing I can do about it." Blaming mother keeps us passive, tied to her. It helps us avoid taking responsibility for ourselves (pp. 43-48).*

Ms. Friday's statement is not only true of the mother/daughter relationship, it is true with regard to any human relationship if it is to be a healthy, productive contribution to society. Focusing upon our conception of the past and spending a large amount of creative energy fiercely defending models which are designed to place blame for the injustices of the past prevents us from being in the position to take advantage of new exciting opportunities. However, examining the past, understanding it, appreciating it for the impacts it has had and capacities it nurtured for our future is a much more productive approach. This is particularly important when we remember that most opportunities tend to present themselves through periodic, often brief, "*windows*" or historical moments.

How can we move past the insanity of being locked into our own "feudal models of reality." How can we stop spending almost all of our time trying to convince ourselves that our "feudal models of reality" *are* reality? In considering these questions, our unqualified answer is that we must "do something positive with what we already know." Such an approach would pose the question in the following manner: *What can we do constructively with what we already know about the history that has brought us to this moment in time*? To answer this question, let's first look at some of the things that we already know.

We know, for example, that no one can do a very good job of driving forward by spending all of his or her time staring into the rear view mirror. We know that everyone has a model of reality, a conceptual scheme that helps the person order his or her perception of the world and make decisions that govern his or her actions. *The Deficit Model* and *The Racism Model*, as we have shown, are two schemes that operate as explanations in the area of *diversity*.

These models might serve us well if we planned to stay in our "feudal castle" for the rest of our lives. However, we will need something else to help us become active participants in an increasingly global world. Whatever we might think or feel about the history of Black people in America, we also know this fact. *Human history converts into time and time into living experience and living experience into skills.* Therefore, the real question of the day is not *if* Black people have something to bring to the organizational table but *what* and *how* can what we bring be integrated with what others bring. How can it be integrated so that it positively contributes to the mission of the organizations to which we belong and to our existence as human beings on this planet.

The true invidiousness of *The Deficit and The Racism Models* is the mythology that they tend to create and perpetuate. This mythology is one that suggests that the model *is* reality rather than a temporary, time-bound perspective or a limited and limiting "social construction of reality" (Berger and Luckmann, 1967). We present other barriers in this chapter but, without some willingness to bring these two insidious models into the light of intelligent scrutiny, most of the others become moot.

Barrier Three: The Degrees of Me

During much of the book thus far we have been talking about managers, employees, executives, academics, Black people, White people, minorities, women, and men. The Degrees of Me barrier brings us back to the most fundamental reality. We are all human beings. As humans beings, we are all blessed with and plagued by one inescapable fact—we are social animals. We should be proud of our individuality and what we can do and accomplish on our own but we, also, have a profound need to associate with, live with, communicate with and gain help from others.

As we live with, work with, play with, and generally associate with other people over time, we tend to develop a range of norms or expected, predictable behavior patterns. Such norms help us immensely in our relationships, interactions and communication with other human beings. Where there is true and frequent interaction between individuals, there usually develops trust and respect and an ability to identify with the others needs, problems, goals, capacities, etc. If we would review the history of Black and White people in America, we would notice that one of the most blatant realities in American history is that there has been a distinct, consistent, and enforced separation between White people and Black people. If trust, respect and a realistic assessment of a person's capability are facilitated by close association, there is no mystery why the *management of diversity* is such a problematic issue in American Society.

The "Degrees of Me" is a concept that helps us focus upon the subtlety of separation and divisiveness as it has occurred in this society. Since "me" is usually defined as "okay," then "you" are only okay to the degree that you look like, dress like, think like, talk like, walk like and act like "me." In a society like the United States of America, which articulates a rugged individualism and the "up by your boot-straps" philosophy, it is ironic to discover the "Degrees of Me" social phenomenon acting as one of the barriers to change. However, from our perspective, the individualistic, "up by the boot straps" philosophy promoted so strongly by Americans is simply mythology. It is mythology for any social animal. Human beings, including the staunchest capitalist Americans, are social animals. The free, capitalistic structure of American society does provide individuals with the opportunity to pursue their personal dreams but the idea "I did it all by myself" is pure fiction.

When the social phenomenon of the Degrees of Me is applied to the social history of separation between the races in America, we begin to understand why it acts as one of the barriers to the development of a multicultural organization. White Americans control all of the major productive and supportive industries in this country. They control manufacturing, medicine and medical technology, communications, education, finance, news reporting, entertainment and distribution. For the moment, we need to suspend any judgement as to whether this reality is good or not. We will accept it as something that simply is. What it means, however, is that white Americans are almost in complete control of the means to create, communicate and sell their conception of what it is to be American. If any of us would take an objective look around we would see that this is exactly what White Americans have done.

The *standard* of beauty and attractiveness in America, while undergoing some recent modification, is still based solidly on the characteristics naturally possessed by White people. English, or to be more specific, the way that it is spoken by educated White Americans is called "standard" and other ways of speaking the language is referred to as "non-standard," if not "sub-standard." The *standard* for demonstrating intellectual capacity is based upon discreet, dichotomous logic, which tends to be the dominant White European mode for acquiring knowledge rather than the concrete, holistic synthesis that predominates in many cultures of color.[39] Say the word "professional" to an American and it means the *standard* of behavior that has become almost synonymous with the way White people have been raised and trained. Displaying other modes of behavior in a "professional setting" means that you are perceived as less "professional."

We could go on but the examples above make our point. It is natural for human beings to feel more comfortable with and to desire to associate with others who have similar backgrounds and are more like them. It is natural for social animals like human beings to want to help, promote and support others with whom they can identify and feel a familiar connection. All these things are normal. However, what seems to have occurred in America, is that the natural behavior and predisposition of the *dominant White culture* have somehow become the "standard" definition for quality, talent, professionalism, etc. instead of being seen for what they are — *the cultural norms of the dominant White American culture*.

One factor that contributes greatly to this type of distortion is the lack of research and study to help us understand the elements of *White American culture*. Go to any reasonably-sized library and you will probably find hundreds, if not thousands, of anthropological studies examining the various aspects of "non-dominant" cultures of all types. Ask the librarian to show you the section where one might find the volumes examining White American culture and you will elicit a blank stare. When we recently asked this very question to the main librarian in the Social Science Department of a large metropolitan library, she first told us that the information would be found in the *History Department*. Later, she discovered two references in her area under the key word WASP.

Now, let's consider some of the negative implications of these facts for non-dominant people of color. The effects of the *Degrees of Me* have worked to the detriment of Black people in America. African Americans neither look like, act like, think like, talk like, or walk like White Americans. African Americans have come from a different historical background and social tradition. We are different people. But, rather than being viewed simply as different people, the "Degrees of Me phenomenon," as it relates to the dominant White majority, has meant that *difference equals deficient.* The most important and most pervasive element of the *Degrees of Me* in America has been the "degree of whiteness" in color or "like whiteness" in behavior.

Judging by the demographic trends that are evident today, the world of the future will be more and more *multicultural.* The past freedom or luxury available to the dominant W*hite American culture* to use its cultural norms as the definition of quality is being reduced daily as we move to the reality of a truly global economy. While most of us will still be influenced by the social forces of the "Degrees of Me" phenomenon, the reality of American life, and the world are that "ME" is beginning to look different. A truly *multicultural world* requires that we learn about the talents and strengths of *all* cultures; that we see them and understand them for the contribution they can make to our existence; and that we work together to integrate these strengths and talents into the *multicultural* fabric of the whole.

Barrier Four: The Floating Criteria

This barrier brings to our attention a number of familiar concepts. *Criteria* are used in performance evaluation. Why do we need to evaluate anyone's performance? One answer might be that we need the make sure that we are getting what we are paying for and to ensure that the person is honoring his/her contract commitments. Another answer might be that there is a "prize" for which people are competing and we need to ensure that the "best person receives the brass ring."

To illuminate this issue, let's use the prize notion just mentioned above. Climbing the corporate ladder or "upward mobility" may be viewed as the "prize" for which members of the organization are competing. Standards and criteria are set so that the organization can ascertain the best qualified person. We believe that most organizations feel that both their standards and the criteria used for evaluation are objective and, therefore, adequate measures of a person's qualification. However, a curious phenomenon occurs almost daily in every organization that we have ever experienced. A simple question is asked by someone to his/her supervisor or manager — "What *exactly* do I need to do to get this promotion or job?" The person may be told about the quality expectations of the supervisor, the specific standards that have been formally set and the criteria against which he or she will be evaluated. Supervisors usually believe that they have answered the question with such responses.

But, if the employee pushes further by asking "Is that everything I need to do?" or by making an "if-then" reference such as "if I do all the things you have outlined, then you are saying I am assured of getting the promotion or job." The supervisor will now start to hedge. Why? If the standards and criteria are "objective" measures of performance and if we want to promote the best performers, why can't we spell out exactly what is required and guarantee the promotion to anyone who is the best performer against the standard. One of the problems, of course, is the shrinking number of positions as one goes up a corporate hierarchy. However, the larger problem is that when managers and supervisors refer to standards they are not really discussing "standards of performance." In the way standards usually operate, they are, in essence, "screening standards."

In other words, these *standards* are used to "screen" individuals from a pool of available applicants so the manager can decide who can be allowed into the organization to perform. Other *standards* "screen" among a pool of competing employees to determine those who will be seriously considered for the promotion. If we listen closely to what we call "standards" and ask the question "to what degree do these standards guarantee a person's actual performance," we often find that there is a low correlation. Again, the standards and criteria create the pool of people who may be given the opportunity to have their performance examined for the promotion or job. Unfortunately, our experience tells us that the actual bases of the decision for a promotion or job are set upon yet another set of criteria. While this set may be inclusive or consistent with the "objective" *standards* stated by the supervisor, they are often unarticulated and "float" depending upon which conditions are important to the decision maker at the time. We have dubbed it as the *FFF criteria* — Friends, Family, and Familiar

The particular elements of the screening standards are set by those who hold the power positions in the organization. How many times does a person work as hard as he/she can to meet and/or exceed the stated standards only to discover that something else was important, but not stated, that prevented his/her achieving the prize. The person may be told that the "timing" wasn't right (e.g., they hadn't spent enough time in the present position or were trying too early, etc); they didn't seem to fit in with the social expectations or were not viewed as a "team player."

Whatever the reason, the essence of the *floating criteria* is that it is a decision making bubble that allows those in power to maintain control over the selection process so that they can choose who they want. These individuals also control the decisions regarding the specific criteria from the "floating set" which will be used to make the actual choice for promotion. We have experienced this as a reality of corporate life. It doesn't say that it will always work to the detriment of Black people, but the power of the *floating criteria* guided by the FFF principle does open the way for unequal distribution of rewards.

The concept of the "glass ceiling" may very well be describing a phenomenon that is a result of this mechanism in operation. The issue of the *glass ceiling* is one in which a person or group is only allowed to rise so high in a company hierarchy before encountering invisible and artificial barriers which prevent them from fulfilling their full potential. One might argue that the individuals in charge deserve the right to evaluate. But, without a broader consideration of the utility of *cultural diversity* and the value that can be gained by the application of the *principle of heterogeneity* in this area, the *floating criteria*, differentially applied will continue to contribute to the creation of *glass ceilings* which screen out otherwise competent employees.

Barrier Five: Pluralism and Performance

Pluralism and performance are a logical follow up on the discussion just completed on the implications of the *floating criteria*. However, this barrier has more to do with the dynamics that occur when we examine the *pluralism* of *cultural diversity* and the "psychology of performance evaluation and human development." The discussion of this issue draws heavily from the arguments made in the paper by consultant J. Howard, *Pluralism and Professional Development: Minorities, Women and the Psychology of Performance* (1988).

America is a pluralistic society. This means that there is real variety and *diversity* in the "stakeholders" of the American dream. Images of the *melting pot* notwithstanding, it is important that we recognize the vital impact of America's pluralism. Whether the *diversity* is based upon culture, ethnicity, race, gender or religion, different groups of Americans have experienced the benefits of being a part of this great country and they will not give up their earned stake in its opportunities.

The opening paragraph of J. Howard's paper is very important in setting the context for his argument and in placing his paper within the scope of this chapter. He writes:

> *Performance and professional development, despite their social and economic importance, have not been*

the subjects of the kind of detailed analysis that could illuminate their dynamics. This lack of serious study is attributable to the tendency in American Culture to view performance outcomes as direct reflections of the characteristics of the performer. Once we have assessed the intelligence or emotional toughness of the individual, what more do we need to predict competitive performance? Indeed, once we know how well an individual performs, are we not in a position to make inferences about the intellectual and emotional endowment of the performer? The very strong tendency in American society to view performance as a simple function of ability is a problem. It not only obscures deeper understanding of performance as a complex phenomenon, it may very well represent an important psychological factor affecting performance in its own right.[40]

J. Howard's objective in this piece is to explore the dynamic social factors that influence performance rather than follow the traditional line and connect it to ability alone. In this way, he is able to focus upon some of the different social dynamics that come into play when we add pluralistic factors such as race or gender to the performance equation. Through such a focus, Mr. Howard goes below the surface and isolates some key factors that operate in the "interpersonal process" of high performance. All other things being equal, it might be permissible to view performance as a simple function of ability. However, "all other things are not equal."

The most important aspect of Mr. Howard's analysis is the vital role that expectancy plays in performance. He offers a conceptual model to illustrate the key relationship. He states that "human beings possess a unique capacity to control one another's actions through the verbal and nonverbal communication of expectations." Research literature spanning many years has well documented the powerful impact of expectancies on performance. Most of us are aware of this connection even if we may not be as aware of all the various ways in which we send and receive signals of expectancy.

The contribution that J. Howard makes is the creation of a model which shows the two areas most directly affected by "credible expectancy." One area is the amount of a performer's effort and the other is the attribution that a performer makes about the reasons for his or her success or failure. If an individual perceives that little is expected of him or her or if they learn to expect little from themselves, it is unlikely that the person will put forth the type of sustained effort necessary to compete successfully with high performers. In addition, if the effort is not put forth and the person fails, he/she is more likely, given the propensity in American Culture, to attribute the failure to a lack of ability. The failure in one situation attributed to ability is likely to affect the "expectation of the outcome" in similar future situations with a corresponding negative impact on effort.

J. Howard's argument suggests that the great disparity in performance between White people and Black people in America, particularly in intellectual and academic endeavors, is much more a product of the dynamics of negative expectation rather than the traditional reasons of laziness or inferiority in ability. J. Howard asserts that the Black response to differences in achievement as racism and discrimination is likewise simplistic. Both views represent a type of finger pointing and they fail to take the responsibility for more objective analysis and problem resolution. The real issue of "pluralism and performance" is the reality of change in the demographic representation in American Society and the lack of corresponding change in our methods and procedures for determining both high quality ability and for assessing the potential for high quality performance.

Barrier Six: Time and Timing-Windows of Opportunity and the Teachable Moments

Time and timing are two barriers that govern every aspect of human life. Perhaps, because time is so pervasive, its strong effects are often overlooked when we examine a situation or event. Since we would not wish to make such an error, we pose the question, "How does the issue of time and timing relate to the *phenomenon of managing diversity* and the social, cultural change which it implies?"

In the process of personal and organizational change, time affects the process in two ways. First, there is the evolutionary aspect of *time,* which simply means "how long" the system has been operating or, in the case of individuals, their age, or how long the person has been living. This is the aspect of time that brings the reality of historical development into the process of social change. When we look at the evolutionary flow of historical events, with respect to the diversity problem, a number of things become evident.

First, it is not very likely that the individuals in history responsible for the economic decision to bring Black people from Africa to America envisioned, or even concerned themselves with, the possibility of the diversity question as it is being experienced today. Second, it is obvious that the number of years and the billions of interactions it took to get us to this place in history cannot be reversed. They are what they are. Third, while we recognize this reality, we also realize that the current situation arrived in small incremental steps. Therefore, the size of the problem should not be used as a reason for failing to act.

It will take the same small, consistent, incremental steps to move things in a different direction. However, it does take a definite decision to act in order to start the time clock and movement in a different direction. This is a final way in which the issue of time affects the process of individual and organizational change. It is the "bounding nature" of time. Everything that we do is "bounded" by time. There is the beginning or start time and there is the ending or stop time. Whether we think of it in such terms or not, this bounding aspect influences and does much to define the success or failure of a change project. Sufficient time assists success. Insufficient time almost always guarantees failure.

For an eloquent discussion of this point see Dr. Ralph Kilmann's book, *Managing Beyond the Quick Fix* (1989). Dr. Kilmann notes that there are simple problems and complex problems. Simple problems may be resolved easily with simple, mechanistic organizational structures, simple methodologies and a short term, "quick fix," time perspective. Complex problems, however, like the issues associated with the *management of diversity*, require complex organizational *paradigms*, complex or integrated cooperative methodologies and a long-term time perspective.

Now, the issue of "timing." The timing issue arises as an integration of the elements and processes of any intended change with the historical reality of time and the *current reality* of time. While this is a convoluted way to express the point, what we are discussing is "the right time" for something to happen. Often the right time is determined by a delicate political balancing act. Conceptually, we represent the issue of timing by two concepts: (1) The "window of opportunity" and (2) The "teachable moment." Both concepts convey the very sensitive or intimate relationship of timing issues to the bounding aspect of time discussed above.

Sense time is relentless, the conditions that create certain opportunities or special moments during which a person is open to receive a particular piece of information won't stand still. It may be that the opportunity or moment will return again but there are no guarantees. The primary reason that the timing issue stands as a barrier is its fleeting character and the reality of the forces operating to cause human beings to postpone or refuse to take necessary action. Throughout history, there have been focal events which signaled the right time for action. In the area of civil rights and race relations, for example, the refusal of Rosa Parks to relinquish her bus seat to a white passenger is now universally recognized as one of these moments. However, even in this famous case, the moment would have been lost without the existence of people who were aware of its significance and willing to take the necessary action to create the opportunity for monumental change.

Barrier Seven: Pressure to Maintain the Status Quo

This barrier is implicit within much of what we have already said in this book. The book focuses upon the topic of *diversity management*. More broadly, the book is about *multiculturalism* and the process of moving an organization to a place where it can be a more effective multicultural entity. The assumption is that by such actions that the organization would be placed in a better competitive position within the global, *multicultural* world of the 21st century and beyond. Thus, as we have frequently stated, we are talking about the processes of social and cultural change.

The classic theorist Kurt Lewin articulated the model for change which has stood the test of time. Today, it is still the quintessential elaboration of the change process. Change involves (1) Unfreezing of the *current reality* or the *status quo*; (2) changing or moving to a new reality and (3) re-freezing or stabilizing the new reality so that it has a similar comfort, predictability and improved effectiveness in comparison with the old status quo. The simplicity of Lewin's model truly understates the extreme complexity of the activities, energy, commitment and planning that is required to complete all three stages successfully in a change effort. Kilmann (1989) elaborates more of the real complexity involved in the change, success process.

What is important to say here is that any organization, whether First or Second Generation, that wishes to move on to the status of a *multicultural organization* must accept the challenge of Lewin's first stage — Unfreezing. We believe that the barriers identified in this chapter are the most formidable elements holding the *current reality* of the *status quo* in place. This is not a quick fix. Diversity programs, however highly touted or profiled, will be like Band-Aids applied to a crack in a flood gate if they don't address, in a systematic way, the barriers we have discussed.

A classic tension has always existed between the requirement to innovate or change in order to survive and the strong desire to hold on to what is mastered, understood and comfortable. The fact that this tension exists as a reality is not an acceptable excuse for the failure to act progressively. Often, we tend to look at the status quo in grand generalities. It is either positive or negative depending on our perspective. The *status quo* is usually positive and something that needs to be defended when we happen to be an integral functioning part of it, and it becomes negative and requiring change when we are locked on the outside of its benefits. From our particular point of view, it is more productive, especially in *diversity management*, to view the *status quo* as simply, "what is." Viewed from this perspective, we accept the status as the current reality and we can then use the "Principle of Deliberate, Continuous, Planned Change" to move the organization forward by developing and implementing the type of systematic processes that will improve the system.

---

[38] In America, it is customary, when making reference to black people to lump them together into the general category of "minorities" which includes all non-dominant groups of color as well as White women. This is the main reason we chose to separate the White woman according to her membership in the dominant white culture.

For Americans, the two most identifiable racial groups associated with the models discussed in this section are White people and Black people. Therefore, we shall speak, specifically, of Black people as we discuss the elements of the models with the understanding that many of the dynamics created by the use of these models apply equally to the experience of other minority groups of color and to White women.

Additionally, as black authors, who share a real part in the dynamics being discussed, we will depart momentarily from the normal detached third person writing style. In this section we will use the more inclusive personal style. We have chosen this direction because we will need to make some critical comments about the responsibility of black people for our models. We, therefore, want it clearly understood that we view ourselves as part of the total collective of black Americans who have to do our part to resolve some of the problems of this country.

[39] Someone has said that the definition of intelligence is the ability to consider two contradictory propositions at the same time. If history is any evidence, White people possess the ability to not only consider two contradictory propositions simultaneously, they can also act upon them and logically justify the contradictory action.

[40] This point is made even more dramatic when we recognize the types of instruments and data that have traditionally been used to determine a person's ability.

— Chapter Seven —

WHAT MANAGING DIVERSITY LOOKS LIKE WHEN IT IS DONE WELL

As we bring this book to its conclusion, we must shift our focus from that of reporting on a phenomenon to making some predictions about the nature of corporate life if we happen to succeed in our efforts to confront the barriers presented in the last chapter and *manage work force diversity*. This chapter will be unavoidably prophetic because there are very few organizations currently operating who fit the conditions we have outlined, and that we believe are required, in order for an organization to claim to be truly *multicultural*.

In a real way, this situation is similar to the old problem of *critical mass* as viewed from the societal level. In the United States of America, we don't have enough organizations, presently existing, to provide us with proper direction and a base of support. There are few organizational role models to help us understand what it is like to be multicultural. It is, therefore, very difficult for organizations at this historical juncture, that is, at the beginning of a new millennium, to visualize what they would look like or what activities would be occurring if they were to cross the barriers into *multiculturalism*.

In considering this problem we have produced the material in Figure 2. The information can be seen as a model that condenses some of the main ideas in the book. The model presents these ideas in a way that may help organizations review their situation in order to determine the degree to

Figure 2

A MODEL OF THE ELEMENTS OF WELL MANAGED DIVERSITY

- Top Management Commitment
- Valuing
- Open Communication
- Equitable Distribution Across All Levels
- Compensation Tied to Achievement of Goals
- Active Mentoring for All
- Education to Teach the Skills of Managing Diversity
- Shared Responsibility
- Planned Careers
- Legitimization of Employee Groups

↓

Good Growth Culture

↓

Some Results

- Low Turnover
- More Comfortable Interactions
- Team Effectiveness
- Knowledge About Different Values and Motivations
- Clearer Vision
- Quality Decisions
- Productivity
- Improved Contribution to the Business
- Competitive Advantage
- No Employee Group Advantaged Over Another
- Recruiting Advantage
- Multi-directional Feedback
- Extends to All Levels of the Organization
- Proactive Responses to Issues vs Reactive
- Mentoring Actively Going on for All
- Visible Role Models for People of Color and Women
- Managing Diversity Viewed as a Continuum vs a Campaign
- Increased Survival Skill for Global Economy

which they are on track toward *multiculturalism*. The first section of the model reveals what we see as the vital prerequisites that must be in place before a proper climate or culture, conducive to human growth, can be approached. If these elements are put in place and integrated into the operation of the business, then a proper climate will exist.

We have argued in this book that becoming a *multicultural organization* is an evolutionary change process. As such, it will contain the classic elements as well as the classic problems of all change processes. As is the case with the change model of Kurt Lewin, the simplicity of our model disguises the tremendous complexity involved in the process of diversity management. The items listed as key elements in the first section of the model are *dynamic* in that they comprise many processes that must be continuously monitored. The final section of the model details some of the benefits we believe will accrue to the organization for its efforts in cultural change.

In this chapter, we will briefly cover the elements shown in the model that we believe are absolutely essential preparatory steps in building the type of culture that will foster personal growth and that will assist the organization in moving toward *multiculturalism*. These elements possess a common characteristic. They possess a quality of flexibility and sensitivity that is an indispensable ingredient in the culture of a *multicultural organization*. The elements are:

- Valuing,
- Open Communication,
- Equitable Distribution Across All Levels,
- Compensation Tied to Achievement of Goals,
- Active Mentoring for All, and
- Education to Teach the Skills of Managing Diversity.

Valuing

One of the most vital yet illusive aspects of an organization doing a good job managing diversity is the concept of "valuing." Valuing means that the people and the organization have the capacity to appreciate and to utilize the multitude of differences, experiences and talents which are brought to the organization by a diverse work force. This is important because, in order for an organization to truly value its people, it must have people who are able to express their valuing of one another and organizational processes and procedures which allow all members to contribute their attributes to the productive process.

This is an extremely illusive element. For too long we have assumed that processes and procedures that have worked for years for one group are good enough for and available to all other groups. It was believed, in error, that once people had been hired or recruited into a company, they had equal access to the developmental and promotional processes so necessary for contributions and progress. The organization that manages diversity well does not make this mistake of omission.

The well-managed diverse organization has managers who realize that a real sense of being valued comes not only from "hearing" but also from "feeling." The person is told his/her value and that he/she belongs to the family, but more importantly, the person feels like a member. This feeling comes from processes and procedures of the organizations that are truly receptive of the differences in people. Such an outcome is intentional, therefore, the well-managed diverse organization does not leave this appreciation to chance.

Open Communication

The area of diversity management is confounded by a maze of miscommunication. People want to know the relationship of *diversity* to *affirmative action*, an area which we have shown already carries a reservoir of confusion, miscommunication and hostility. To get a good sense of the kinds of concerns raised by managing diversity programs see the questions in chapter nine of *Beyond Race and Gender* by Dr.

R. Roosevelt Thomas, Jr. (pp.167-182).

In view of the propensity for miscommunication associated with diversity issues, companies managing it well will have a strong component of open communication. Questions and concerns from employees will be viewed not as challenges to the program but opportunities to "get the word out," to clear up misunderstanding and to build involvement and commitment throughout the organization toward the direction it is moving — a functioning multicultural system.

Equitable Distribution Across All Levels

The well-managed diverse organization will have an equitable distribution of this diversity across all levels of the organization. It is not enough to say that Black people are "statistically representative" when the diversity is skewed to certain (often lower) levels or in particular functions or occupations. True diversity means that what is good for lower level workers of the company is also good for the executives.

This is not a small point because executives of well-managed companies know that their behavior signals their real goals and objectives. They can talk all they want about how important something is to the organization, but if that importance is not reflected in the behavior of the managers throughout the organization, the rank and file will know what to do with the message.

Unfortunately, this is one of those points which touches on the sensitive issue of hiring quotas. It has been a highly charged, emotional issue for a number of years and any organization that plans to exist in the multicultural environment of the future will have no option but to face and resolve the controversy in order to formulate an effective approach to the problem. If an organization is not currently diverse, the only path is to initiate progress through some distinct phases similar to those we have presented in this book. We already know that in the first generation of successful hiring and promotion activity, issues of reverse discrimination, special treatment, unfairness and quotas will arise. But, well-managed companies "manage their business" and do not allow their business to "manage them." The same principle is true of well-managed multicultural organizations. They manage the issues that arise in the process of cultural change and they don't allow themselves to be trapped into inaction by the forces attempting to maintain the status quo.

Compensation Tied to Achievement of Goals

It is probably axiomatic in business organizations to say that people pay attention to "the things they have to count and the things that count." Inventory is not a foreign concept to business managers and any good manager knows the importance of keeping track of and control of the organization's inventory — the accounting for resources that have to be counted. While not often viewed this way, an organization's human resources can be understood as its inventory of vital skills and abilities which allow it to conduct its business effectively and to interact with the other organization resources to achieve the company's purpose or that which counts.

Organizational goals and objectives are the means by which an organization steers itself toward its purpose. They are a primary means for integrating and directing the organization's human resources in accordance with organization needs. The overall organization objectives will not change for the organization that is successfully managing diversity. However, in such organizations there are distinct production goals with appropriate accountability systems and distinct human resource maintenance goals with appropriate accountability systems. In addition, there must be a system for communicating the importance of this dual set of goals for the organization. The idea of linking compensation to the achievement of production and people management goals is an important component in an effective managing diversity program.

Active Mentoring for All

Having a well-managed diverse organization demands that we bring a vital aspect of all successful organizations out of the closet and into plain view — the process of mentoring. Recently, it has become more acceptable to discuss this process in the career development of every employee, but it has always been important. Prior to the introduction of the concept of "Minority Affirmative Action" that openly exposed the need for active mentoring of minorities and women, mentoring was a more subtle, selective process which we could refer to as the "Corporate Affirmative Action Program" for fast-track White males.

If diversity is to be managed well, this vital process must be active, continuous and available to all employees. Active mentoring will be one of the most difficult elements to put in place in the well managed diverse organization. It is difficult because an effective mentoring process is not something that can be legislated. You can't simply assign everyone a person who has the responsibility of mentoring and expect that the work will be done. Mentoring within organizations is part chemistry and part response to the climate existing in the organization.

In our model, the existence of active mentoring for most employees could be viewed as a "results" item that indicates how well the key change variables have been implemented. However, we have placed it among the key elements because it is an area that should not be left to chance. The well-managed diverse organization of the future will have to have in place well-developed mentoring processes as a way to ensure the integration of talented individuals from all sectors into the organization.

Education to Teach the Skills of Managing Diversity

It might seem that an organization doing a good job of managing diversity would not require an education program to teach the skills. Excellence in the management of diversity is an evolutionary process which takes time to master. The historical patterns of educational, employment, socio-economic, and housing experience that helped to create our ignorance about issues of diversity are not likely to change soon. Companies committed to the effective management of a diverse work force recognize this and continues to educate their employees in the skills necessary to function in a multicultural environment.

Additionally, education concerning diversity is necessary because the issues stemming from developing a diverse environment also evolve and become more complex. These are not the types of issues which can be "fixed" once and, then, forgotten. Issues of difference will continue to present difficult puzzles for managers and other employees. Continued education helps provide a proper forum for facing some of these issues and a mechanism for discussing and developing processes for preventing future problems from interfering with the organization's productivity.

CONCLUSION

There is much talk these days about the realities of American society as we have witnessed the close of the 20th Century and the birth of the 21st Century. There are concerns about quality education, the effectiveness of government, the rapid expansion of information technology, the environment and, of course, the age-old concerns about race and gender. As complex and confusing as this mosaic of issues already is, one thing in every camp seems very clear — the speed of the change will continue to accelerate as we move further into the 21st Century. This book has revisited one of the major topic areas in the *mosaic of change* in American society. We have examined the general topics of race, color and the interaction among Black people and White people, particularly with respect to the corporate or the work sector of America.

When we began this project, our primary focus was on the need to contribute to the growing literature addressing the challenges of managing work force diversity and creating effective multicultural organizations. We have worked in many related areas for years and feel that we have something useful to say. While our agenda is still pretty much the same, we discovered in the process that there were some serious blocks to the achievement of our objective. One barrier was the ambiguity and misunderstanding surrounding many of the key concepts. Another was the lack of common perspectives among different racial groups and the strong emotion that is usually generated by any discussion of race and color in this country.

We began the project with a sincere desire to offer some of the acquired knowledge from our experience which we felt would help clarify some of the misunderstanding that seems rampant in the discussion of the topic of cultural diversity or multiculturalism. We were pleased with our work at the conclusion of the initial draft, that is, until we were confronted with the question of the degree to which a group of Black people, speaking primarily from the perspective of their own experience in corporate America, could be considered representative of "multiculturalism."

We went through draft after frustrating draft, trying to rid the book of this dilemma. While each draft was better than the preceding one, each one remained impaled upon the horn of the same dilemma. The final resolution came as a result of reviewing Dr. Andrew Hacker's powerful book *Two Nations: Black and White, Separate, Hostile, Unequal* (1992). Dr. Hacker faced a similar dilemma in approaching his work. His response to the dilemma is captured by his quote:

> *The book's title might seem to intimate that a full portrait of America can be rendered in black and white. Obviously this is not the case. While persons we classify as black or white still comprise America's major races, they currently account for a smaller share of the population than at any time in our history. Since we want a full perspective, Asians and Hispanics and other ethnic groups will obviously appear on these pages.* ***Still,*** **Two Nations** ***will adhere to its title by giving central attention to black and white Americans, and the reason for this emphasis will be made evident. In many respects, other groups find themselves sitting as spectators, while the two prominent players try to work out how or whether they can coexist with one another*** [p. xii, emphasis ours].

The main learning that we derived from our review of Dr. Hacker's work can be gleaned from three phrases in the quotation above: (1) *giving central attention to Black and White Americans*; (2) *other groups sitting as spectators*; (3) *the two prominent players try to work out how or whether they can coexist with one another.*

While many of the things we have said in the book will have some application to the experience of other minority groups in the multicultural mosaic of America, our concern has been with the implication for the relationship between Black and White Americans. More specifically, we have been concerned with ending the negative, non-productive, "game playing" nature of the relationship between these two groups.

We find ourselves in agreement with Dr. Hacker's assertion that Black people and White people are the *two prominent players* in the game of American race relations. We also believe that the game is a destructive one that must stop if we seriously plan to have any more than a minor role in the truly global economy toward which the world is destined. We hypothesize that, in order to stop playing the familiar game of "pretend race relations," we must first understand some of its structure, its nature and the various parts Black people and White people play in its maintenance.

Once this was accomplished the key question became, "What do you do with the knowledge that is gained from such an examination?" This is where Dr. Hacker's second phrase helps us. Our decision was to use the information we discovered through our experience and our skill to fashion a strategy which Black people might employ to effectively "kill the race game." The strategy can be stated simply: *Black people can kill the race game by a conscious decision to end the part we play in supporting and maintaining it.*

As Black professionals who have come to maturity within the racial caldron of America, we have decided to examine that experience, to analyze it conceptually, and to say what we think will have to be done if we are serious about either ending the game or changing its direction. The discussions in this book have been, in essence, an open interchange among Black people about the things we need to do to stop promoting the game. We have touched on certain historical facts that have negatively impacted our experience as Black people in America. We have analyzed these historical realities from a unique economic perspective that allows us as Black professionals to focus our attention on the economic consequences for us today. It was from this perspective that we made some prescriptions concerning what ought to be done.

Now that we have come together to reveal the results of our collective experience of more that thirty years in White dominated corporations, the real question is, "So what?" We have condensed this learning into a compact book that tries to loan the reader our eyes and the perspective on multicultural issues that has been developed through our experience over the years. Again, we ask, so what? Who really cares about the views of five minor characters on the vast world stage of global multicultural complexity? Can anything be learned from this collection of new voices that has not already been covered in the writings of the past great minds of our time? What are we really to make of this "game theory" approach to the serious business of diversity management and evolving multiculturalism?

We don't know if we have the *best* answers but it is critical that we provide the answer that has been derived from our experience. This book represents over thirty years of experience for each of its authors in the "killing fields" of programs and activity of corporate diversity management or the lack of it. As clearly articulated in one of the articles in the appendix, Black people have been and still are on the point in the struggle for racial justice. It is also reasonable to expect that those of us living today are likely to conclude our natural lives at this *point position.*[41] Since it is likely that we will not see the conclusion of the war, we courageously accept our lot, as millions of other Black people have done in the past, and we do what we can to weaken the strength of our adversary's stronghold.

Our role, the role all point people in the war of cultural diversity implementation, continues to be to provide the critical intelligence necessary in order for the advancing army of our children and grandchildren to have a chance at victory. It is the kind of victory that is embodied in the liberation song *We Shall Overcome.* It is a victory that would be exemplified when reality is consistent with Dr. Martin Luther King Jr.'s dream, when Black people are truly judged by the content of their character and not the color of their skin. This is the real "so what" of this book. The key question is, "What are you going to do to help end this sickness?"

The time for playing the race game is over. The time for acting as if we don't possess the skills or the resources to end this barbaric attack on our humanity is over. Almost 400 years ago (if we use 1619 as the starting point), the serious economic game of using Black people as a major component of the economic engine of America was set into motion. We were judged to be perfect for the task. We came from a distant land and a distant culture. In heritage, we were distinctly different from the dominant culture, the people who wanted to use us for their benefit. If White people conceived of themselves as good, benevolent, industrious and manifestly destined to master the world, it was easy to cast us as bad, naturally sinful, lazy and, therefore, needful of their benevolent leadership. The most critical factor in this economic exploitation process was the fact that we possessed the immutable characteristic of black pigmentation. With this genetic characteristic, there was no way to hide, no way to slip out of the slave designation once it had been assigned based upon the Black color of our skin.

The effectiveness of the color tactic is so strong and so beneficial to the exploitive agenda of White people that when we talk about any program designed to redress past injustices inflicted on Black people, the one thing that White people refuse to allow is the connection of the redress solution to the immutable criteria of our Blackness. In other words, to implement the system of injustice, America used color but it will accept almost any other designation except color to redress the problem. The main problem with this approach is that it was the criterion of color that sealed our fate and it is this same characteristic that is used to maintain a system of benefit for White people to the continued detriment of Black people. Unless we understand this, we will continue to construct weak redress programs based on concepts such as "minority status" that water down redress strategies by including a wide variety of other groups that never were forced to endure what color delivered to us.

What does it mean to say that the time for playing the race game is over? Are we not ourselves, by continuing to recount the 400 years of negative history as if no progress has been made, still playing the same game? Yes, this would be true if our main motivation for writing the book was to continue the game of beating up on White people for the sins of their fathers. But, that is not our purpose or our motivation for this book. Our goal has been clearly established in our minds and in the arguments we present in this book. Our goal is to kill the race game altogether by refusing to play our part.

To help explain our position, let us recount an incident that occurred during a discussion among Black people who were discussing the need for economic development strategies in a large African American section of a median sized Midwestern city. One person felt that understanding the impact of 400 years of mistreatment of Black people in this country was very important if we were going to solve our problems. The other person argued that the past was the past and what we needed to do now was to forget the past and focus on the future. Our position is that the argument itself is a remnant of the divisive tactics that were implemented as part of the race game.

When two Black people disagree about the impact of history on the lives of Black people, one saying it is very important and the other saying that we should ignore it and focus on the future, they both are correct in one sense. Assuming both people are really concerned about improving the condition of Black people, the one who said that history is unimportant is correct in that an overly "emotional reaction" to any historical event is a useless waste of creative energy. However, the person who said that history was very important is correct in that "intellectual or analytical proaction" with respect to any significant set of historical events is absolutely essential to future progress.

Constantly reacting in an emotional manner, be it the sad moan of lost nostalgia or the passionate hostility of disgust, keeps us in a race game whose rules are controlled by our adversary and sustains the game as a current negative force in our lives. However, an opposite effect can be achieved through an intellectual analysis of the historical components of the game and interventions designed to dismantle its structural supports. Such an approach focuses our attack and directs all our creative energy and effort toward the agenda of our own self-interest. We simply stop doing the dominant culture's work. We refuse to stay locked into a reactive system that always placed us in the position of responding to an agenda that is set by other people.

We believe that, apart from everything else, the main reason for the enslavement of Black people was the fact of its economic advantage. We believe that the physical attribute of our distinctive color was the primary component for selecting us as slave objects. Additionally, although in direct contradiction to America's stated creed of individual freedom, it is another historical fact that religious, legal and political principles and processes were put into place or set in motion to justify our treatment. These facts have acted together to produce severe limitations on our ability to function as effective citizens in this country. It has produced the insidious structure of the race games that we now say it is time to dismantle. So how do we suggest that we do this and how can the information provided in this book assist in the process of this liberation agenda?

First of all, we have to realize that, as much as the information that produced our problem is based in historical fact, that is only one side of the historical analysis. It is also true that the information that forms the basis for a resolution to our problems is based in the same set of historical facts. What are some of these facts?

1. It is a historical fact that we, through the biological linage of our African ancestors, come from the stock of people who were kings and queens.

2. We come from an African ancestral heritage that is strong in its spiritual and cultural roots. If we stopped focusing on the negative accounts of our history that the dominant culture continuously attempts to force upon us, we could discover clear evidence of our spiritual and cultural strength. For example, if we use the date of 1619 as our historical beginning in America, we would see that we have been subjected to the dominant culture's attempts to dehumanize us for over 350 years. There was first outright slavery and denial of freedom, then legal slavery and then de facto slavery. Now that we have fought to end outright slavery, entire economic institutions, mostly beneficial to the members of the dominant culture, have been established to cure the illness in our people that was caused by these practices.

3. Yet, given all these facts of history, given all that we have endured, we still are here. We have survived. Some of us have done very well in a system that was designed to enslave and restrict the opportunity of

all of us. The one fact that this alternative view of our history reveals is that there is no way that the racism game can defeat us, that is, if we remember the strengths imbedded in our history and spend all of our time and all of our resources focused upon an agenda that is in our group self-interest.

The emotion laden *Deficit Model* will suggest to us that such a stance is impossible. It will say that we have been physical and psychological slaves too long. It will say that there is no chance to change our condition. However, it is our position that a sustained intellectual focus on the positive facts of our history would suggest a totally opposite answer. True multiculturalism is not only in our self-interest, it is in our hands. Black people and other non-White people of color do control the levers for turning this society into one that truly lives up to its creed. While it seems strange to view it this way, this country actually needs our input for its very survival. It is time to stop being or acting "less than" and to stand up and make the contributions that only we can make.

If you are a Black CEO, make sure that your organization is one of quality and that it embraces and reflects the type of determination and spiritual quality that has been demonstrated throughout the history of our people. As proclaimed in the title of Mr. George Frazier's book — *Success Does Run in Our Race.* If you are a Black person working in Human Resources for any corporation, act as a real professional by ensuring that the company's published statement, "We are an equal employment opportunity company," is not just a statement of legal compliance but one that is realized by its policies, practices and results.

If you are a Black history professor or a Black professor of anthropology, begin to help the dominant cultural group understand itself by conducting major studies on its culture. White America is the one cultural group in America where there is an absolutely dismal amount of research literature. It is really ironic to hear White people promote themselves as the leaders of America's cultural assembly when, in fact, they are the one group who would have a very difficult time defining who they are or documenting the existence of their culture in the libraries of America. When you subtract the ethnic Whites from this group and the peoples of color that the census takers have defined as White, the only people left are those who are just White. Who are they? Where did they come from? What is their ancestral heritage? What are their cultural values? What qualifications do they really bring to the multicultural table?

Finally, if you are a formally uneducated mother or father of Black children, please understand that you still possess skill. Begin to acquire some of the formal credentials you need so that the lack of these symbols don't continue to be the *stated reason* for a race conscious system to deny you a proper evaluation of your skill and your potential. If you are a Black person who has chosen to inoculate your senses with drugs or alcohol, understand who you come from and that millions of your ancestors gave up their lives so that you could have the choice of life or death. We hope you will cease the death march, choose life and join us by making your contribution to real life in America.

This book stands as a challenge to the whole process of game playing in the relationship between Black people and White people. It is true that the book focuses its discussion mainly upon one group but the objective remains the same. As is true with any type of two-party game or competition, if one side refuses to play its part or to follow the prescribed rules, the competition dissolves. If there are White people interested in ending the racial game, the book can be helpful by stimulating thought and a similar kind of dialogue among White people. When White people understand the ways in which their structures, procedures and behavior help maintain the race game, the remedy is the same. Interested

White people can also end the game by refusing to continue the traditional script.

Before we close our discussion in this book, we need to make some comment about an issue that will almost certainly come up as a result of some of the ideas we have presented. It is the issue that our book will only promote more *divisiveness* among the races rather than promoting a "spirit of unity." This is an issue that tends to surface with virtually every discussion of the race situation in this country. There are many people who feel that any discussion of the racial situation in America is divisive. We are not so naïve as to think that we will eliminate this criticism by making a few comments, but we do believe that a few statements are warranted given our serious belief that this book can contribute to more unity among the races.

Once, while attending a racially mixed Bible study group, the topic of unity among the races was brought up. One of the participants, after listening to the conversation for some time, remarked that he felt there was "a big difference between the phrase *the spirit of unity* and the phrase *the unity of the spirit.*" As we continued to reflect upon and discuss these two expressions, a clarifying thought was proposed to the group: "The *spirit of unity* is *acting like* we are . . . and the *unity of the spirit* is *being what* we are." In this context, the *spirit of unity* is expressed in the plaintive cry by Rodney King, "Can't we all just get along?" It is the spirit that has been proclaimed by ministers, both Black and White, from the pulpits of so many Christian churches in America.

These ministers have encouraged their congregations to "establish a program of interfaith worship with a neighboring Black or White church in order to fellowship in a spirit of unity and brotherhood." It is the same spirit that may have influenced the Founding Fathers to write into our Constitution the words, "We hold these truths to be self evident, that all men are created equal . . ." The *spirit of unity* is not a bad spirit because it is often promoted by good, honest people who really would like to see the country come together.

The main problem with the expression *spirit of unity* is not its intent. The problem is that the criteria for judging its achievement seem to be satisfied even if we simply *acted as if we were united.* For example, in the good *spirit of unity*, many White people and some Black people say that we should be "color blind" in this society. And, we seem to be able to do a pretty good job, given the particular circumstances, of *acting like* we are color blind. However, there is nothing that is truly color blind in American society. Acting as if we are color blind in this instance is still fantasy; it is still a game.

The phrase *unity of the spirit,* on the other hand, is qualitatively different. Its focus is not on *acting like we are* but rather *being what you are.* Human beings are equal in that they possess potential that can be developed. Those of us who are Christian understand Christ has one body, one spirit, and that we are all a part of that body and spirit. We are already united in spirit. In the physical sense, Christians may be Black or White; politically, they may be liberal or conservative, Republican, Democratic or Independent; in terms of their denominational affiliation, they could be Baptist, Presbyterian, Catholic or a number of other denominations from A to Z. But, if they are Christian, that is, if they have done the one thing God requires for rebirth into His family, they are already part of His one body.

The relevance of these comments is that in this book we propose to speak to those who share a *unity of the spirit* and to encourage our readers to *be what they are.* Black Americans *are* Americans. Black Americans, as Americans, are free to think, speak and act in accordance with the rights and privileges granted to all Americans. This book encourages Black Americans to use their acquired positions and status in America to focus on group self-interest, as does every other American racial group, and to act upon those interests. Group self-interest is not necessarily a denial of the unity of the whole. America is a republic of immigrants. The diversity in that heritage is not our weakness but a good source of our strength. It is simply not true, as is often asserted, that a focus on group self-interest is divisive by nature.

As co-authors of this book, we have had personal experience with the unifying power of *being who we are.* This project brought five unique individual Black professionals together to say something about ending racial games. We were three males and two females; we came from different geographic areas and different socio-economic backgrounds; we represented different philosophical perspectives. In short, we were and are very different people and, occasionally, our minor differences would arise and threaten to negatively affect the project.

The attacks would come from the usual invidious spirits of divisiveness such as *ego, male chauvinism*, *misinterpretation* and *misunderstanding,* or notions such as, "It's my way or no way." We survived these attacks and completed this project because we recognized that *we are of one spirit.* By focusing on that reality, we were able to identify and work through the difficulties created by our differences. Our prayer is that God will bless this project by allowing the *unity of His spirit* to shine through so that we *plural but equally human Americans* can work through our issues by *being who we already are.*

The world of the 21st Century requires that we put down the games that keep us apart and focus our time and energy on resolving the problems that face us all as human beings.

Lessons from Geese

As each goose flaps its wings, it creates an "uplift" for the bird following. By flying in a V formation, the whole flock adds 71% more flying range than if each bird flew alone. Lesson: People who share a common direction and sense of community can go further and get where they are going quicker and easier because they are traveling on the thrust of one another.

Whenever a goose falls out of formation, it suddenly feels the drag and resistance of trying to fly alone, and quickly gets back in formation to take advantage of the "lifting power" of the bird immediately in front. Lesson: If we have as much sense as a goose, we will stay in formation with those who are headed where we want to go.

When the lead goose gets tired it rotates back into formation and another goose flies at the point position. Lesson: It pays to take turns doing the hard tasks and sharing leadership — with people, as with geese, interdependent with others.

The geese in formation honk from behind to encourage those up front to keep up their speed. Lesson: We need to make sure our honking from behind is encouraging — not something less than helpful.

When a goose gets sick or wounded or shot down, two geese drop out of formation and follow it down to help and protect him. They stay with the goose until it is either able to fly again, or dies. Then they launch out on their own with another formation or catch up to the flock. Lesson: If we have as much sense as geese, we will stand by each other like that.

—*Author Unknown*

---

[41] A full discussion of the thesis of the "point position" is contained in the paper, "Stemming the Tide of Black Professional Suicide: A Call for Point People," in the Appendices.

REFERENCES

Alderfer, C.P., Alderfer, C.J., Tucker, L., & Tucker. R. (1980). "Diagnosing Race Relations in Management," *Journal of Applied Behavioral Science*, 27: 135-166

Aldrich, J.W. (1987). "How Black Managers Can Compete," *Management Review*, 76: 28-30.

Anderson, Claude. (1994). *Black Labor, White Wealth: The Search for Power and Economic Justice.* Edgewood, MD: Duncan, Inc. Publishers.

Baird, L., & Kram, K.E. (1983). "Career Dynamics: Managing the Superior/Subordinate Relationship," *Organization Dynamics*, 11 (4): 46-64.

Berger, P.L., & Luckmann, T. (1967). *The Social Construction of Reality*. Garden City, New York: Anchor Books.

Bergmann, B.R. & Krause, W.R. (1968). "Evaluating and Forecasting Progress in Racial Integration of Employment," *Industrial and Labor Relations Review*, 399-409.

Bhagat, R.S. (1979). "Black-White Ethnic Differences in Identification with the Work Ethic: Some Implications for Organizational Integration," *Academy of Management Review*, 4: 381-391.

Bowens, H., Sims, R.R., & Veres, J.G. (1987). "Tactical Actions: Surviving Organizations," *International Journal of Management*, 4(3): September, 457-469.

Breeden, James O. (1990). *The Slave Master: The Ideal in Slave Management in the Old South.*

Brown, H.A., & Ford, D.L., Jr. (1977). "An Exploratory Analysis of Discrimination in the Employment of Black MBA Graduates. *Journal of Applied Psychology*, 62: 50-56.

Business Week. (1980). "Corporate Culture: Those Hard-to-Change Values that Spell Success or Failure," October 27: 148-160.

Campbell, B.M. (1990). "Success Beyond the Open Door," *Black Enterprise Publication*, 21: 112-114.

Conklin, R. (1968). "Ethnography." In D.L. Sills (ed.), *Encyclopedia of the Social Sciences*, New York: Free Press.

Copeland, L. (1988). "Learning to Manage a Multicultural Workforce," *Training*, May 48-56.

Cose, E. (1993). *The Rage of a Privileged Class.* New York: Harper Collins.

Cox, T.H. (1991). "The Multicultural Organization," Academy of Management Executive, May.

Cox, T.H. & Blake, S. (1991). "Managing Cultural Diversity: Implications for Organizational Competitiveness," *Academy of Management Executive*, 5(3): 45-56.

Cox, T.H. & Nkomo, S. (1986). "Differential Performance Appraisal Criteria," *Group and Organizational Studies*, 11: 109-119.

Crotty, P.T., & Timmons, J.A. (1974). "Older Minorities — [road-blocked] In the Organization," *Business Horizons*,17(3): 27-36.

Dalton, Harlan L. (1995). *Racial Healing: Confronting the Fear Between Blacks and Whites.* New York: Doubleday Dell Publishing Group, Inc.

Davis, G., & Watson, G. (1982). *Black Life in Corporate America: Swimming in the Mainstream.* New York: Doubleday.

Deal, T.A., & Kennedy, A.A. (1982). *Corporate Culture*. Reading, MA: Addison-Wesley.

Dickens, F. Jr., & Dickens, J.B. (1982). *The Black Manager: Making It in the Corporate World*. New York: AMACOM, A Division of American Management Associations.

DiTomaso, N., Thompson, D.E., & Blake, D.H. (1986). *Corporate Perspectives on Minority Advancement in Management*. Paper presented at the 46th Annual Meeting of the Academy of Management, Chicago.

Dyer, D., Dalzell, F., and Olegario, R. (2004). *Rising Tide: Lessons from 165 Years of Brand Building at Procter & Gamble.* Boston: Harvard Business School Press.

Etsy, K. (1988). "Diversity is Good for Business," *Executive Excellence*, 5: 5-6.

Ference, T.P., Stoner, J.A.F., & Warren, E.K. (1977). "Managing the Career Plateau," *Academy of Management Review*, 2: 602-612.

Fernandez, J.P. (1975). *Black Managers in White Corporations*. New York: Wiley.

Fernandez, J.P. (1981). *Racism and Sexism in Corporate Life: Changing Values in American Business*. Lexington, MA: Lexington Books.

Friday, Nancy. (1977). *My Mother / My Self: A Daughter's Search for Identity*. New York: Delacorte Press.

Gerber, B. (1990). "Managing Diversity," *Training: The Magazine of Human Resources Development*, 27, (7): 23-32.

Greenhaus, J.H., Parasuraman, S., & Wormley, W.M. (1990). "Effects of Race on Organizational Experiences, Job Performance Evaluations, and Career Outcomes," *Academy of Management Journal*, 33 (1): 64-86.

Hacker, Andrew. (1993). *Two Nations: Black and White, Separate, Hostile, Unequal*. New York: Ballantine Books.

Harlan, A., & Weiss, C.L. (1982). "Sex Differences in Factors Affecting Managerial Career Advancement." In P.A. Wallace (Ed.), *Women in the Workplace*. Boston: Auburn House, 59-100.

Haro, R.P. (1991). "So-Called Experts on Cultural Diversity Need To Be Subjected to Careful Scrutiny," *The Chronicle of Higher Education*, November 13, B2-3.

Harris, A.S. (1990). "Second to One: Second-in-Command Executives," *Black Enterprise Publisher*, 20: 278-280.

Hill, Anita F. and Jordan, Emma C. (Ed) (1995). *Race, Gender and Power in America: The Legacy of the Hill-Thomas Hearings*. New York: Oxford University Press.

Hill, N. (1960). *Think and Grow Rich*. New York: Fawcett Crest Books.

Hymowitz, C. (1989). "One Firm's Bid to Keep Blacks, Women," *Wall Street Journal*, February 16.

Ilgen, D.R., & Youtz, M.A. (1986). "Factors Affecting the Evaluation and Development of Minorities in Organizations." In K. Rowland & G. Ferris (eds.), *Research in Personnel and Human Resource Management: A Research Annual*. Greenwich, Conn.: JAI Press, 307-337.

Irons, E., & Moore, G.W. (1985). *Black Managers in the Banking Industry*. New York: Praeger.

Jackson, B. (1975). "Black Identity Development," *Journal of Educational Diversity and Innovation*, School of Education, University of Massachusetts, 20-25.

Jackson, S.E. (1989). "Team Composition in Organizational Settings: Issues in Managing a Diverse Workforce." In *Group Process & Productivity*, J. Simpson, S. Warchel and W. Wood (eds), Beverly Hills, CA: Sage Publications.

Jamieson, D. & O'Mara, J. (1991). *Managing Workforce 2000: Gaining the Diversity Advantage*. San Francisco, CA: Jossey-Bass Inc.

Johnson, W.B. (1991). "Global Work Force 2000," *Harvard Business Review*, March-April.

Johnson, W.B., & Packer, A.H. (1987). *Workforce 2000: Work and Workers for the Twenty-first Century*. Indianapolis, IN: The Hudson Institute.

Jones, E.W., Jr. (1973). "What It's Like To Be a Black Manager," *Harvard Business Review*, 51 (4): 108-116.

Jones, E.W., Jr. (1986). "Black Managers: The Dream Deferred," *Harvard Business Review*, 64 (3): 84-93.

Kanter, R.M. (1979). "Differential Access to Opportunity and Power," In R. Alvarez (ed.), *Discrimination in Organizations*. San Francisco: Jossey-Bass, 52-68.

Keeley, M. (1980). "Organizational analogy: A Comparison of Organismic and Social Contract Models," *Administrative Science Quarterly*, 25: 339-362.

Kilmann, Ralph. (1989). *Managing Beyond the Quick Fix.*

King, F. (1977). *Wasp, Where is Thy Sting?* New York, NY: Stein and Day Publishers.

Kraiger, K., & Ford, J.K. (1985). "A Meta-Analysis of Race Effects in Performance Ratings," *Journal of Applied Psychology*, 70: 56-65.

Kram, K.E. (1985). *Mentoring at Work: Developmental Relationships in Organizational Life*. Glenview, IL: Scott, Foresman & Company.

Lawrence, P. (1975). "How To Deal with Resistance to Change." In *Harvard Business Review on Management*. New York: Harper & Row, 390-405.

Leinster, C. (1988). "Black Executives: How They're Doing," *Fortune*, 117: 109-110.

Levitin, T., Quinn, R.P., & Staines, G.I. (1971). "Sex Discrimination Against the American Working Woman," *American Behavioral Scientist*, 15: 238-254.

Loden, M. & Rosener, J. (1991). *Workforce America: Managing Employee Diversity as a Vital Resource*. Homewood, IL: Business One/Irwin Press.

Mai-Dalton, R.R., & Sullivan, J.J. (1981). "The Effects of Manager's Sex on Assignment to a Challenging or Dull Task and Reasons for the Choice," *Academy of Management Journal*, 24: 603-612.

Mandrell, B. & Kohler-Gray, S. (1990). "Management Development that Values Diversity," *Personnel*, (67) March: 41-47.

Merenivitch, J. (1990). *Model: Stages and Benefits of Diversity Management.* The Procter & Gamble Company, Food and Beverage Division.

Merenivitch, J. & Reigle, D. (1979). *Toward a Multicultural Organization*. The Procter & Gamble Company, Industrial Relations Division, Cincinnati, Ohio.

Mobley, W.H. (1982). "Supervisor and Employee Race and Sex Effects on Performance Appraisals: A Field Study of Adverse

Impact and Generalizability," *Academy of Management Journal*, 25: 598-606.

Naisbitt, J., & Aburdene, P. (1990). *Megatrends 2000*. New York: William Morrow & Company, Inc.

Nemeth, C.J. (1986). "Differential Contributions of Majority and Minority Influence," *Psychological Review*, 93: 23-32.

Ouchi, W.G. (1980). "Markets, Bureaucracies, and Clans," *Administrative Science Quarterly*, 25: 129-141.

Ouchi, W.G. (1981). *Theory Z: How American Business Can Meet the Japanese Challenge*. Reading, MA: Addison-Wesley.

Pazy, A. (1986). "The Persistence of Pro-Male Bias," *Organization Behavior and Human Decision Processes*, 38: 366-377.

Perkins, D.N.T., Nieva, V.F., & Lawler, E.E. III. (1983). *Managing Creation: The Challenge of Building a New Organization*. New York: John Wiley.

Pfeffer, J. (1981). "Management as Symbolic Action: The Creation and Maintenance of Organizational Paradigms." In L. Cummings & B. Staw (eds.), *Research in Organizational Behavior*, Vol 3. Greenwich, CT: JAI Press.

Schwartz, F. (1989). "Management Women and the New Facts of Life," *Harvard Business Review*, January/February: 65-76.

Sodano, A.G., & Baler, S.G. (1983). "Accommodation to Contrast: Being Different in the Organization," *New Directions in Mental Health*, 20: 25-36.

Solomon, C.M. (1991). "Are White Males Being Left Out?" *Personnel Journal*, November: 88-94.

Songer, N.B. (1991). "Work Force Diversity," *Business & Economics Review*, 37(3): 3-6.

Steele, S. (1990). *The Content of Our Character*. New York: St. Martin's Press.

Thomas, D.A., & Alderfer, C.P. (1989). "The Influence of Race on

Career Dynamics: Theory and Research on Minority Career Experiences." In M.B. Arthur, D.T. Hall, & B.S. Lawrence (Eds.), *Handbook of Career Theory*. New York:Cambridge University Press, 133-158.

Thomas, Jr. R.R. (1990). "From Affirmative Action to Affirming Diversity," *Harvard Business Review*, 2 (March/April): 107-117.

Thomas, Jr. R.R. (1991). *Beyond Race and Gender: Unleashing the Power of Your Total Work Force by Managing Diversity*. New York: AMACOM/American Management Association.

Triandis, H.C., Hall, E.R. & Ewen, R.B. (1965). "Member Homogeneity and Dyadic Creativity," *Human Relations*, 18: 33-54.

Trost, C. (1990). "Women Managers Quit not for Family but to Advance their Corporate Climb," *Wall Street Journal*, May 2.

Van Maanen, J. (1979). "The Fact of Fiction in Organizational Ethnography," *Administrative Science Quarterly*, 24: 539-550.

Wallace, A. (1972). Paradigmatic Processes in Culture Change," *American Anthropologist*, 74: 467-478.

Williams, R. (1990). *They Stole it But You Must Return It*. Rochester, NY: HEMA Publishing.

APPENDICES

Key Papers Discussing Additional Concepts and Arguments

(NOTE: There is some repetition in the first two papers — "Offensive Tactics in the Face of Covert Racial Discrimination" and "Living and Growing in Hostile Cultures." The ideas and strategies in the papers were first developed and presented in the offensive tactics paper and designed for a specific problem being experienced by Black military recruits. Later, the strategies were viewed as relevant and applicable for a more general issue of survival in hostile cultures. Therefore, they were rewritten and presented in the "Living and Growing in Hostile Cultures" paper.)

Appendix 1

OFFENSIVE STRATEGIES IN THE FACE OF COVERT RACIAL DISCRIMINATION

By
Howard Bowens, Ph.D.

OFFENSIVE STRATEGIES IN THE FACE OF COVERT RACIAL DISCRIMINATION

This paper will address the question of how a person can use his particular and unique character system to devise helpful strategies for dealing with many of life's problems. The particular focus of the paper is on the problem of covert racial discrimination. However, I believe the general ideas are applicable to other areas as well. The notions that are presented in this paper are extremely powerful because they are dealing with very powerful processes in the dynamics of life. The reader should consider thoughtfully the ideas presented in the essay. The fundamental premise is based upon a deep interest in the pursuit of knowledge of self.

Before proceeding further with this paper, I would like to return to a summary of the fundamental ideas presented in a previous paper — "The Elements of a Black Man's Character." These important ideas will form the conceptual structure for the strategies and tactics that will be discussed later. In "The Elements of a Black Man's Character," I tried to articulate the results of many years of thought and introspection concerning my own personality development. Much of the impetus for the thought had come from some painful experiences where I seemed to lose sight of myself and to drift into periods of depression and others of elation. Much of my early life had been a consistent experience of relative success and personal satisfaction in my achievement. My achievements caused me to progress and somehow I reached a point where all the strategies and ways of behaving that had proven so successful before no longer seemed to work. I was scared by this and I was determined to find out what had gone wrong. As a result, I became a subject in my own analysis.

I learned that for me, and I believe for every other human being as well, the character structure is composed of three basic elements:

(1) A basic thrust or focal issue.
(2) An orienting conceptual system.
(3) Strength.

The *basic thrust* is the fundamental issue a person is dealing with throughout his or her life; it is the issue that sends the person into a tailspin of fear, irrational behavior and anxiety whenever it is truly threatened or the person believes that it is being threatened. At these times the person's whole life seems to be in jeopardy. The *orienting conceptual system* is the place where the person's values are manufactured. It is also the guidance system that helps the person select the kinds of experience in life that are likely to be most consistent with his or her basic thrust. In other words, it helps to "discriminate" among those experiences that are most likely to build his or her sense of self and give the most satisfaction and the least amount of frustration and pain. *Strength* is simply the knowledge of self and the will to do what one needs to do in order to maintain a strong self-confidence. It is interesting how easily this statement rolls off the tongue. I wish the knowledge I am referring to was acquired as easily.

Definition of Key Concepts

According to *Webster's Dictionary of the American Language,* "prejudice" is defined as a "strong feeling for or against something, formed without any knowledge or logical reason; especially a general antagonism toward members of other races, religions, etc." A man by the name of Terry has devised a very practical formula which realistically defines another key concept — "racism." Terry's formula says PREJUDICE + POWER = RACISM.

In descriptive terms, Terry's formula means that racism exists when a person or collective unit uses power to support and implement specific prejudices as defined by Webster. I believe that the formula is also useful when dealing with other "isms" in American society, such as "sexism," "classism," "anti-Semitism," etc. "Discrimination" is the behavioral activity which results from prejudice and racism.

The question is how do these definitions relate to what I have already said about a person's character system and, more generally, to the topic of covert racism. Webster's definition gets at my basic point when it says that prejudice is "feeling" formed for or against something without knowledge or logical reason. All human beings are prejudiced and I believe that the basis for each person's particular brand of prejudice is the primary socialization process everyone goes through prior to the age of five.

The processes of socialization during these formative years are powerful and they are subtle, and backed by the inescapable force in the person's need for parental protection and love. Given the nature of the primary socialization process and the time at which it occurs, a literal fact is that all of us emerge from the period with strong discriminatory feelings that we have little knowledge of nor logical reasons for. We react all our lives to stimuli related to this early training and, much of the time, we are unable to articulate why we behave as we do. We say things like, "It's my nature," or "That's the way I am," or any number of other phrases to describe in general terms something we are unable to pinpoint specifically.

The reader will recall that we are laying the foundation for discussing offensive approaches to *covert* racial discrimination. The term covert carries with it the negative connotations of maliciousness, deviousness and deceitfulness. These are not the meanings that I wish to associate with the principles outlined in this paper, but the people who need to understand what I am saying will undoubtedly encounter examples of discrimination in their lives that fulfills all of these negative connotations.

The image I wish to convey by the term *covert* is that the acts of discrimination are not obvious or clearly visible. Their affect may be the same as *overt* discrimination but the person is not necessarily aware that he or she is doing anything wrong. This view is more consistent with what I have already said and I am convinced that it is more consistent with the majority of life's experiences. The point is that people discriminate against other people. Also, people who are in control of institutions set up practices which reflect their values and, therefore, systematically discriminate against other people who do not happen to share these values or who don't seem to share them. Much of this is done with very good intentions in mind.

The Tactical Principle

There is one big problem with the kind of "no fault" definition of racial discrimination that is the basis of this paper. In our culture we are so used to viewing our way of life in such benign terms that when something goes wrong, we tend to associate it with a *culprit.* "The values we hold and the way we do things are okay, the problem must be in the fallibility of the human animal." We can easily become immobilized when faced with problems which cannot be traced to *something* that *someone* does wrong. Culpability we understand, but we are frustrated and immobilized in the situation of no-fault.

Basically, I think that to work effectively and consistently on the resolution of problems created by covert discrimination, the person must be able to get beyond "blaming." The attitude that I wish to convey is described very well by Nancy Friday in her book, *My Mother/My Self* (pp. 83,84). It is at the very end of her second chapter ("A Time to be Close") and she apparently realizes that her readers may be so caught up in the power and pain of her description of mother/daughter symbiosis that they could miss a vital point for the book. She says:

> *In the name of fairness, and reality too, let me add an important postscript which is true not only for this*

chapter but of this whole book: looking over our shoulder at what mother may or may not have done so many years ago locks us into the past. 'She did it. There is nothing I can do about it.' ***Blaming mother*** *keeps us passive, tied to her. It helps us avoid taking responsibility for ourselves.*

'One of the major resistances in analytic work,' says child psychiatrist Aaron Esman, 'is the notion, 'It was my mother's fault.' Patients don't want to see their own responsibility, so they blame mother. In our post-Freudian world, it's very fashionable, but to blame mother means one doesn't have to examine one's self, to face one's own problems. Parent-baiting, mother-baiting uses up energy that might better go into examining the wrong choices one has made oneself.' Brooding over past injustices, we have little emotion left over to create a better future.

The same thing is true of us Black people when we concentrate too much of our time, emotional energy and discussions on the previous injustices that have been largely responsible for our current plight. No one can deny that these injustices occurred and that they have had a profoundly damaging effect on the development of our race. But, Ms. Friday says, blaming the past helps us avoid taking responsibility for ourselves and this is the real issue for the future development of any people. How do we do this?

I believe that moving to a position where a person starts to take responsibility for themselves requires difficult preparatory work. The person is leaving the dependent, child-like world of reasonably secure direction that is given by others. Taking responsibility for yourself means creating your own world view and running the risk that others won't agree with you; it means a lot of thought about who you are and what you want and a lot of hard work devising the strategies and tactics that will gain you these things. However, above all, it means being willing to do these tough things with the full knowledge that you might fail (or succeed, which we sometimes find even more threatening) and that there is no one who deserves a bigger share of the blame than yourself.

As a young Black man, as I began to take responsibility for my own actions in the face of discrimination, the points made in the above paragraph became very real for me. I needed a new world view, new strategies and different tactics. As I learned more about what was essential, especially the need to be addressing "reality" more often than what I "desired reality to be," I devised a simple tactical principle:

> *I must "know" and "realistically accept" what is. "Accept" in this context does not mean necessarily that I must agree with what happens to be. It means that I must recognize and listen to what my senses tell me about the reality of my environment. The simple principle I try to follow is this: "I may have to lie to others about what I think and feel but I will never lie to myself."*

It is not likely that racism in the American society will end prior to my death. That is a reality and it is one that I must accept and effectively deal with or I will not be able to develop beyond the particular limitations that are set for me by racial stereotypes. Some readers will say, "But don't you think that things have gotten much better?" Historically speaking, of course they have, but, relatively speaking, I am not as sure, and both of these "realities" must be accepted.

In 1979,[42] while White men were desperately seeking new challenges to make their lives more fulfilling, Black men, Black women and White women were still experiencing the "pioneering firsts" in many of the same areas that white men have almost perfected. All of the above, I believe, are real aspects of the American society in which I have to live out my life. Since I am Black, these realities will definitely affect my personal and professional development; this is inescapable. However, it is not true that these realities will determine me in any specific or patterned way. I do have some choice in the matters of my life and I choose to take personal responsibility for the way my life goes.

Strategy: The Pre-Work to Tactical Action

It is one thing to say that I choose to take responsibility for the direction for my life and entirely another issue to actually do it. You have to fight forces within yourself that you never knew existed and sometimes you have to face the frustrating reality that these forces are stronger than you are. You try with all your might to be different in some ways but find it is as fruitless as trying to climb a 90-degree incline with greased hands. Such fundamental parts of yourself need to be accepted for the moment even if you haven't the slightest idea of what is going on within you. Learn to trust the reaction of your body, it is more true than your rationality.

There are some parts of yourself that can be worked on and changed with success and an accompanying feeling of exhilaration. However, just as in the case of military combat, to win you must have a "game plan," a guiding strategy which organizes your resources into effective tactical action. You must be supremely prepared for the struggle you are about to be engaged in, including the critical information about such things as the nature of your opponent, knowledge of the opponent's strength and weakness, knowledge of your own vulnerability, etc. I like to use the imagery of war when dealing with this subject because I believe it is appropriate in almost all of its dimensions.

Racism wounds people psychologically just as badly as an M16 will wound a person physically. Racism cripples and can even make vegetables out of people. Make no mistake about it, the analogy is real. "Overt" racism is analogous to conventional warfare and "covert" racism is analogous to "guerrilla" warfare. One responds to at least some set of logical rules and is a bit more tangible and rational. The other responds only to the rules of the moment and these rules are set by the opponent with the most power for the situation being confronted. The only sane way to deal with guerrilla conflict is to train your senses, your intuition and the speed of your reaction time. You have to do some very funny things with your values also. Below are some specific points which I feel help a person become prepared for scuffles with covert discrimination.

(1) First, you must analyze and examine the components which maintain and give substance to what is the current reality in the system. For example, if it is organizational racism we are talking about, we must take a look at such things as the numbers of minorities, the positions people hold, the way the work is done, the expectations around social behavior, etc. You must refrain from allowing your particular values to interfere with this analysis of "what is" because the cleaner this description, the more useful it will be.

(2) Second, you must analyze and "really know" yourself. By this I mean, you must be willing to accept all that you know and learn about yourself even though some of those things may not be very pleasant. Such a bank of knowledge will enable you to become sensitive to and identify where it is that you are a "realistic misfit" in the normal social realities of the organization.

Discrimination is a very emotion-evoking phenomenon. In essence, it is rejection in one of its most subtle yet brutal forms because the rejection is not based on a realistic assessment of the person being rejected. There is not much that the person can do to correct the situation because he or she can't change the physical characteristics that have been given negative associations. It is a "no win" situation and it brings out the kind of erratic behavior and hostility that is usually associated with acute frustration. When the discrimination is covert there is frequently no objective means for addressing it. Therefore, there seems to be no logical or reasonable justification for the erratic, sometimes hostile, reaction of the person feeling the discrimination. This is what makes covert discrimination so insidious. In order to reach some explanation, people resort to statements such as "That's the way they are" or worse, "What else would you expect from a person with their background?" These comments don't explain anything. They simply help support the self-fulfill prophesy that has already been established. The really unfortunate part of this situation is that the victim, through his or her uncontrolled reaction, has also contributed support to negative beliefs.

Perhaps now the reader can understand the phrase "really know yourself" in a way that is not readily apparent from the explanation above. To react more effectively in the emotion laden situation of discrimination requires that a person have a good sense of his or her emotional "triggers." We don't normally get to know ourselves in this way but such knowledge is essential to the victim of racism or any other "ism." I have found that the image of a puppet on strings is a good one for helping me become more aware of my emotional self.

As I would experience various strong, emotional reactions to situations, emotions that I couldn't seem to check, I would label it and represent it as a string coming out of my back. This was a way of facing the reality of my vulnerability to certain situations because there was no way I could resist a reaction when someone or something was manipulating one of these strings. However, I learned that I could reduce the negative emotional effect by owning that part of myself. It seemed as though people could only enjoy manipulating others when it remained disguised and denial kept the manipulation underground.

A quick example may be helpful. As a kid I was ashamed of my broad nose and thick lips. These were symbols of ugliness. Any of my peers could reduce me in status just by the mere reference to these features. As long as I tried to deny what *was,* they had the upper hand. One day when a peer made reference to my nose and lips, I said, "My, you're observant," and suddenly his power over me was lost. I have worked hard to get to this place with most of my other strings. It is more than recognition; there must be realistic acceptance of these parts of oneself.

(3) **THIS IS A MOST CRUCIAL POINT!!!** The difference in the cultural or social requirements of a system and the natural assets you have obtained from your own primary and secondary socialization experiences is your "perceived deviance." People in the organization will make assessments of your productive value based on the perceived match between the system's priorities and your assets. Another way of saying this same thing is that this difference will represent your *predictable powerlessness.*

This idea is the crux of this paper. Discrimination occurs when we are dealing with a situation where there is likely to be an important conflict of values or orientation. Many of the discriminatory actions of people are designed to effect what they consider to be a more workable, problem-free blend among people who have to work with one another for some particular purpose. Covert discrimination, or what can also be referred to as institutional discrimination, occurs when the procedures and institutional practices are such that they create more difficulty for one group than another. Sometimes this is intentional and, in other cases, it is not but, as we have said earlier, the effect is the same because this is an issue which impacts the emotional side of the personality.

The reason that point (3) is crucial is that it is a way by which a person can predict beforehand the likely way a system will respond to him or her. The assumption here is that, if a person is aware of a potential situation and if he or she can see its "systematic," non-personal components, there is a greater chance that he or she can maintain a more proactive and productive stance, one that is likely to help him come up with a reasonable solution for himself even if it is isn't optimal.

To explain my point, let me take an example from my military experience which was the place where I had the opportunity to test some of the notions that I have presented in this paper. I was a procurement officer in the Coast Guard's Third District Office and was responsible for the success of the minority recruiting effort. We were making good progress, but I soon began to realize that there was an unfortunate "unintended consequence" for our success. I was stationed at a training base and began to see the fruits of our efforts populate the various schools on the base. I was quite interested in how "our" students were doing and was pleased to find that, on a relative basis, the students were doing okay academically. However, the picture was not as pleasant with regard to "military bearing" or conduct. There was a disproportionate number of Article 15 violations of the Uniform Code of Military Justice by the Black trainees as compared to the White.

When I looked into the situation I received a number of explanations for the problem, but the most consistent feeling among Black trainees was that nobody was paying any attention to their needs and that the White non-commissioned officers who ran the schools were unfairly discriminating against them. It was hard to discern what was really happening but when unexplainable acts of violence began to occur on the base I knew that something had to be done.

After a period of time building the trust and confidence for myself among the Black enlisted trainees, I began to get a better sense of the dynamics that were occurring. The Black students felt that their needs and concerns were not being addressed fairly. Arbitrary rules would be established, they felt, which were designed to prevent them from relating to and expressing their heritage and background. There were rules added to the base's dress codes, prohibiting or restricting the wearing of Dashikis (a popular African-style garb) at the time when no such restriction was placed on cowboy apparel. The students felt that they were frequently harassed in their rooms for playing their music too loud and they were resentful at the seemingly distrustful reaction Whites would have when there were gatherings of Black students. Even such things as the lack of Black cosmetics in the base PX contributed to the feeling of being ignored.

The more I examined what was going on, the more I realized that the problem was due to the natural differences in the way of life for the young Blacks and the old military "salts." The Black students were right in their feelings that they were uncared for and discriminated against because the behavior and attitudes which were important to them were not the norms of the base. The base's leadership was doing what it felt was most appropriate because it was its responsibility to train and shape the students into effective functioning parts of the military system. They did not see any discrimination in their actions because this was their job and they would do the same to any trainee who violated the rules of the system as many Black students were seen as doing.

Because of this situation, there was unfair treatment on the base, and the Black population was experiencing real discrimination. However, the discrimination was "covert" in the way I have described the term earlier. The White officers, non-commissioned officers and petty officers who were responsible for the training of students were not aware of the discriminatory effect of their actions.

When we were able to articulate for them what was occurring and what could help to resolve the situation, the recommendations sounded like the military system was being criticized, as if we were trying to get "special favors" for Black students who were unwilling to honor the commitment of their enlistment contract. We talked a lot about these issues in an effort to come to some understanding of one another and to reduce the frustrating emotional pressures that were helping to escalate situations to the point of physical violence. We were being successful at the rational level.

The base commands were willing to sit down and talk about what was happening, but they were very resistant to entertaining any solution other than one which would result in an answer to what they felt was the "real" problem — *The Black students simply had to learn to accept the fact that this was a military organization and that compliance to the rules and regulations was paramount regardless of how different it seemed to be from their normal environment.* We had a serious dilemma and, at this point, a couple of other points came into play:

(4) When you understand the perception which others may have of you based upon your "fit" with the important values from the system, you have a choice to make. Either you can attempt to draw yourself closer to the system by assimilating its values or you can try to change these values or you can leave physically or otherwise "cop out." The point here is that **YOU HAVE A CHOICE AND IT IS YOU WHO CONTROL THE DIRECTION OF YOUR EXPERIENCE THROUGH THAT CHOICE.**

(5) If you decide to act, then it is a matter of clarifying what it is that you want to do and how you want to go about it and what will be required in order for you to pull it off. It is at this stage where your personal values must be brought back into the picture and used to condition your action choices. Action must have integrity to be sustained so it is crucial not to engage in actions which violate fundamental values which you hold. If you fail to heed this basic point, your actions simply will not be very effective. At times this will be a very difficult principle to follow because your values will not always support the actions which your analysis deems most appropriate for the particular situation.

In reaction to the situation briefly described above, Black students could be seen behaving in all the ways outlined in point (4). Those who made choices other than assimilation were considered deviant in varying degrees and disciplined in accordance to the severity of their offense. Students were getting suspended from school, transferred and some were sent to the base brig. Some were even discharged because of their behavior. It was my belief that many of these students were being disciplined because of their emotional reaction to a situation which seemed untenable.

Since I was having very little success in getting the system's leaders to understand and appreciate what I was trying to convey to them about the problem, I decided to try to influence the approach being taken by the young Black servicemen. By this time I had developed some trusting relationships with some of the key members of the group and they were very significant in helping me to gain the trust of the majority of the group. I was able to present them with the idea that the problem we were facing was not the Coast Guard's problem. The Guard could exist with or without our involvement. But, since we were a part of the organization and the military was not a company that you could easily quit, we had to take responsibility for our own needs. As an officer on the base, I was in a position to gain some resources for activities, as well as add some legitimacy to our programs. Plus, I was the only one with the time to devote to the problem of communication and coordination. The process of the change from blaming the military organization for the frustration of our needs to taking on these things for ourselves consisted of a confrontation of two basic questions:

(1) What, specifically, did we want done?

(2) What did we need to do to reduce the strong negative emotions which were causing so much frustration, causing people to react erratically.

The first question was much easier than the second. It amounted to saying what we wanted and then doing a reality check on the feasibility of getting it done, given our current resources. These were the resources we controlled within our group which meant that to do what we wanted didn't necessitate initial approval from the command structure. It also meant that we could present our ideas when they were formed as a complete package which would include our assessment of the problem, what we wanted to do about it and how we proposed to achieve our desires, given the resources available. The one remaining element which we needed from the command structure was sanction and support. This was a very successful approach but I still do not think it would have worked as well had we not been able to deal with the second, tougher question.

Earlier I used the puppet metaphor to describe a technique that had been helpful to me in getting in touch with my emotional self. I thoroughly believe now, and at the time, that this kind of sensitivity to self is vital if a person is to maintain a more consistent and even emotional state in the face of frustration. The problem was that I did not see that it would be appropriate or effective to try to give the young Blacks a lecture on the merits of this principle. However, I could devise some strategic suggestions for them which were based on the principle and which I felt would work. My thought was that, if the students could experience some success in this area, they would be more able to understand the importance of what I would be saying about the principle underlying the tactic.

One problem that Black students were continually experiencing in the different commands was the issue of "insubordination" to superior officers and petty officers in the performance of their duty. It was happening so often and causing so much anger that I decided that this was the area where I needed to make my point. A big part of the problem was caused by the fact that the military system expects a certain kind of obedience to orders from officers and others in responsibility.

The necessity for this type of obedience is well understood when we think of the combat situation. However, you can't just turn this kind of response on an off at will so it is important for the military system to reinforce this behavioral response even during peace. I have no basic disagreement with the logic in this position but what was happening all too frequently was that the difference in values and backgrounds between Black trainees and their White petty officers created the appearance of insubordination more often than its actuality. Insubordination was being redefined in terms of a "good" and "bad" attitude or "showing *proper* respect," etc.

Too many Blacks were going to Captain's Mast (judicial court proceeding) for these kinds of offenses. My tactic for addressing this consisted of three general parts. First, there was the need for information. I began to hold classes with the students on the nature and structure of the Uniform

Code of Military Justice. The young men had to understand why they were getting into this kind of trouble so often, as well as their individual rights within the code. Once they began to get familiar with the way the code was structured, they began to see how easy it was to be found in violation of the code and this helped them to see the importance of being able to control their emotional reaction to people who were superior to them in the military structure.

The second step was to set a measurable goal. We decided on the goal of reducing the number of masts that Black students were experiencing and, at the same time, to try to increase the number of occasions that students taken to mast on phony grounds would be exonerated. Two things were important to accomplishing these goals:

(1) We used our right to have character witnesses in our hearing. Sometimes we would take as many as 10 or 15 witnesses into such a session. This had the effect of reducing the indiscriminate "railroading" that too often occurred.

(2) I told each student to get a small notebook and to use it whenever they felt irritated at a superior for some kind of unfair treatment. I told them they could write "I love my mother" because it didn't matter what they wrote in the notebooks as long as they didn't say anything out of place. I also expected this small act to be effective in reducing some of the illegal needling because petty officers engaging in this type of behavior depended on a lack of documentation of their behavior.

We found that the number of times students were caught in the former situation of insubordination was drastically reduced. This meant that the number of disciplinary masts were also reduced. The students felt good about what we were able to accomplish and soon we were devoting the majority of our energy to productive activities that were gaining us the things that we had wanted to see on the base for so long. I was truly amazed at the change in the confidence and the positive optimism in their outlook. I think the best way to explain this change is to say that the students were experiencing a new sense of power and potency. This brings me to the concluding points I want to make about the use of offensive tactical action.

Tactical Action

With the decision to act and an idea of how you want to proceed, you are now ready for the creation of the "means" or the tactics for implementing your desires. Below are some useful ideas to consider prior to engaging in tactical action.

Four Important Considerations for Successful Tactical Activity

(1) When anyone engages in the process of tactic implementation, he or she must accept the fact that they are entering into a "power game." It doesn't have to be a very serious power game but it is a game nonetheless and you must realize that you share an equal part of the responsibility for its creation and the repercussions which stem from it. Moral rationalizations or expressions of benign intentions are irrelevant behaviors because once power forces are released by a tactic, it will be responded to positively or negatively regardless of the initiator's specific intent. **THE CRUCIAL POINT AT THIS STAGE OF THE PROCESS FOR THE PERSON SEEKING POWER IS THAT HE OR SHE CRITICALLY ASSESS AND DEFINE WHAT IT MEANS TO "WIN."** Without such an assessment "a priori,"

the person will not be able to get a sense of directed progress toward the objective. The person will also be less able to understand and control the natural expansive nature of all the power games.

(2) There are many forms of power. Everyone has some form of power which they control and are able to use for their benefit. The person seeking more power must have a good sense of which forms of power he or she controls and which ones they do not; he or she must know which forms will aid and which ones, for particular reasons or circumstances, will not be helpful. Every power form has a source and certain situational limitations. The really smart tactician will always take care to learn how to read these situational limitations. In other words, in the natural course of a power game, you must be able to discern when it is time to "eat crow." It is my belief that you must learn how to enjoy these periods as if you were dining on a rare delicacy. You learn more from the *crow-eating* sessions than you do from the *victory dance*.

(3) A person acquiring new forms of power or using his or her resources to gain access to other areas has to keep in mind where "home base" is located. This is the place where the person has the birthright of unconditional support I talked about earlier. It is the place where the person can rest and regroup; a place where the tactical defenses so necessary in the power game can be relaxed. It is important to keep this home base in mind because, as the person moves out into other power arenas, there is the possibility that he or she may be forced

to engage in some behaviors that will be experienced by members of the home-base support group as a violation of some basic values. This will tend to have an affect similar to that of "burning the bridges behind an advancing army." If this, in fact, happens, the person is really in trouble in the balance of the power game. Cut off the source of rest and recuperation and strength, the person will be worn down and defeated in the same way that an army cut off from the support of its home base is worn down.

(4) The final consideration in tactical action is an identification of the specific resources a person has at his or her command and to reach a determination of how to best deploy these resources for the greatest effect. Whatever direction a person chooses to focus the resources under his control, it is key that they be arranged so that they are used to achieve a very specific goal which relates to another specific goal at a higher level which relates to another goal at an even higher level and so on. This type of tactical structure will widen the person's perspective into an overall strategy and will provide him or her with the sense of controlled progress. Under this system, any tactic which fails to achieve its objective will be viewed as losing only one of the battles in the war and not the whole war.

One Vital Caution: Now Let's Get Back to Reality

Taking offensive action against the racism imbedded in an organization requires the acquisition and utilization of personal power and influence in an organizational system. The only people I know who are concerned about the acquisition of power are those who don't have as much as they would like. However, there are real reasons why a person doesn't have power at any particular point in time. There is also no guarantee that the person will be able to keep the power he or she acquires. Power is a fluid, moving entity and it requires constant, critical evaluation, as well as honest "respect" for its potency. There can be no arrogance where power is concerned because its balance shifts with the dynamic mix of interpersonal interaction. A year before writing this article originally, I made this note in my diary.

> *There is no arrogance, there is only stupidity. The stupidity of the arrogant who believe that power is limited by their perspective and control. The stupidity of the powerless who always look to the powerful for guidance as if they had all the answers. Without 'humility', it is only the blind leading the blind.*
>
> — H. Bowens
> October 6, 1978

The following quotation from Carlos Castanada's *Tales of Power* is a most profound elaboration of what I have highlighted in the brief statement above: *True humility is the key ingredient for maintaining a proper respect for power.*

> "... A warrior takes his lot, whatever it may be, and accepts it in ultimate humbleness. He accepts in humbleness what he is, not as grounds for regret but as a living challenge. It takes time for every one of us to understand that point and fully live it. I, for instance, hated the mere mention of the word 'humbleness.' I'm an Indian and we Indians have always been humble and have done nothing else but lower our heads. I thought humbleness was not in the warrior's way. I was wrong! I know now that the humbleness of a warrior is not the humbleness of a beggar. The warrior lowers his head to no one, but at the same

time, he doesn't permit anyone to lower his head to him. The beggar, on the other hand, falls to his knees at the drop of a hat and scrapes the floor for anyone he deems to be higher; but at the same time, he demands that someone lower than him scrape the floor for him ... I know only the humbleness of a warrior, and that will never permit me to be anyone's master."

(The words of Don Juan, page 27)

---

[42] The ideas in this article were first drafted in 1979. However, as I now experience life in 2005, the situation being discussed still exists and the ideas are still relevant.

Appendix 2

LIVING AND GROWING IN HOSTILE CULTURES

By
Howard Bowens, Ph.D.

LIVING AND GROWING IN HOSTILE CULTURES

This is the third section or component to a descriptive process leading to the articulation of what this author sees as the true nature of organizations and highlighting the various implications for the human beings who will be part of organizations. The first component to this process was entitled "Organizations as Neologisms." In that paper we attempted to describe organizations as "complex and constantly shifting configurations of human relationships and socially constructed meanings." Organizations are not physical entities that can be manipulated and handled. Instead, they are dynamic constellations of complex social processes that must be perceived and understood.

The second component of this explanatory process was the ideas expressed in the paper, "Theory and Method of Internal Organization Consultation." This paper comes as close as we can to describing what is viewed as the "essence" of an organization. It details the generic components that comprise most organizations and shows how these components relate with one another and interact to form the "essence" or culture of the organization. The second part of that paper dealt with the process of organizational intervention and change. This was important because we must have a planned mechanism for developing organizations if we are to improve their function of responding to critical requirements in the environment. However, as the reader probably noticed, the nature of the change methodology described in that paper is consistent with our definition of organizations. To change organizations in a planned, effective way, it is necessary that we direct our focus and attention to the "real" organization.

Now we are ready for a third component in the process. If organizations are what we have described them to be and if people need organizations to "survive in a hostile world," we must say something about the nature of the human experience inside organizations. We must try to understand something about the character and source of the forces and influences that are exerted upon the individual. This will help us to understand the various kinds of behavior that we observed within organizations and it may help us develop successful means for ensuring that the forces operating within an organization are directed to enhance individual growth rather than to diminish it. This happens to be one of our fundamental values and it also explains why we believe this component is a vital part of the process of organizational elaboration.

Each of the three sections has its own level of complexity and each has presented specific difficulties to our intention to describe them. This section will perhaps be the most difficult. In many ways we will be talking about the shady or shadow side of the organization; we will touch on the use and misuse of organizational power; we will need to highlight the intended and unintended attacks on human personalities which can do so much damage to some individuals. In short, we will say something about why people in organizations need to think and plan ways to protect themselves from the very system that is a primary source of their identity, development and economic survival. What is it about organizations that demand that we pay attention to such issues?

Some Key Assumptions

Any theory or logical argument is based upon a set of basic assumptions. These assumptions provide the supportive rationale for the actions that are implied by the theory. In the two papers mentioned above we proposed a specific perspective about organizations and suggested some actions based upon that perspective. But what are some of the underlying assumptions that support our prescriptions?

One important assumption is that organizations are human conceptualization designed to achieve the ends of their creators and/or developers. These creators are people who are attempting to deal with real human concerns, desires, aspirations, etc. That is, they are people who use organization to deal with emotion laden needs and goals which are highly associated with their past experience. We further assume that the designs which the entrepreneur or developer constructs (their rational structures) will inevitably incorporate and reflect their underlying emotional concerns. In this respect, the employees or members of the organization can be said to be working within the *emotional constellation* of the organization's founders. Obviously, there is an evolutionary factor which must be considered for those organizations that have existed over time, but at this point we will keep the analysis as simple as possible.

Another key assumption is the notion that groups of individuals differ characteristically as a function of their historical experience. For example, with the historical reality of racial segregation and discrimination in American life, Black people can be said to posses a *characteristically* different experience from White people. As far as organizations go, the difference in the experience of Whites and Blacks is acutely evident with regard to the roles that each has played within them. White males created and still dominate most of America's organizations and institutions. These "establishments" drive, support and define the character of American society. Black people have played a role in this development but not normally as the entrepreneurs, originators, planners and directors. For the moment, we are not concerned with the normative question of whether this has been "good" or "bad" or whether things ought to have been this way. We are simply trying to establish what our experience tells us is true so that the basis for our assumptions about organizations can be made explicit.

Based upon what we have just said about the historical experience of Black people in organizations, one logical conclusion is implied, based upon our assumption about the true nature of organization. Black people and any other minority group in organizations are working within the "emotional constellation" of the dominant White male framers, developers and managers of these systems. One hypothesis that may be derived from this assumption is that the difference in the historical experience between Whites and Blacks in organizations will produce a variety of conflicts and problems. There will be misunderstanding, confusion, misinterpretations, misrepresentation, suspicion, caution and a great deal of uncertainty.

But these generalist statements could be said about what occurs in all organizations, even those that have absolutely no Black people as well as those Black organizations that have no White people. This is very true and it helps us make the point that it is not the racial issue that is the important point of our discussion. The issues that surface due to the racial differences and the historical treatment of race in America are only important to us here because they help to isolate and highlight the particular aspects of human experience in organization that is the thrust of this paper. All organizations experience, to some degree, the conditions we have listed above. These conditions stem from the differences in the basic experiences and the corresponding emotional needs of individuals working together to try to satisfy a number of different personal concerns. Often, these underlying concerns are covert.

We need to reiterate the point above because it is so crucial to the understanding of human experience in organizations, Blacks, women, minorities, etc. are not the only people who have to be sensitive about their position in organizations or careful about their overt behavior. Everyone below the level of the major decision-makers of the system have to be careful and watchful. This is true because everyone below the top levels of the organizations is living within structures that have been established around the rational and emotional concerns of the organization's leaders. And, as we have said, these structures are closely associated with the past experience of these leaders.

We believe, as does Laing *(The Politics of Experience),* that no person's experience is or can be the same as another. All individuals have emotional concerns that stem from and are connected to the uniqueness of their experience. The basic differences in individual experience are enough to create the kinds of conditions that we mentioned earlier. However, individuals from more common social-educational-geographical-temporal backgrounds posses a number of common resources which allow them to have a better chance at resolving the issues that are created by their individual differences.

For example, people from a similar background have a wider range of common metaphors, expressions and they can use many more specific examples to communicate the shades of difference in their overall emotional concern. Where the historical experience of individuals is further apart resulting in reduced interaction, this is less likely to be true. Thus, the primarily segregated social, educational, political and economic experience of Black people and White people means that we are not only further apart in our specific emotional concerns but we, also, have fewer resources to draw upon as aids in communicating about the differences which exist. Another implication of this is that there exists a "magnitude of difference" in the impact of the organizational forces we have highlighted when we consider the racial factor.

Let us carry the analyses of the racial factor in organizations a little further as a tool for highlighting the impact of human differences in general. The differences between Black people and White people with regard to organizational and cultural experiences create and support the many forms of subtle mistreatment, lack of real communication and discrimination. As the cumulative effect of these impacts builds over time, we refer to the ubiquitous result as *racism.*

Racism is not an easy phenomenon to identify or deal

with. A short definition from *Webster* refers to it as, "a belief that some races are by nature superior to others and, therefore, this justifies 'discrimination based upon such beliefs.' " Taking a short associative leap we can use this definition to explain something that could be called "hierarchicalism" in organizations. This concept would refer to the belief that some people at certain levels of the organization or in certain jobs within the organization are, by nature, superior to others. This, therefore, would justify discrimination and certain kinds of mistreatment. People near the top of the organization can fall into the trap of believing that they are inherently smarter than those in lower parts of the system. They, therefore, may fail to utilize the total available brainpower and resources in the resolution of organizational problems. This is a kind of organizational or hierarchical bigotry.

Most of us are familiar with references to bigotry, racism, sexism, classism, anti-Semitism, etc. in terms of conscious attitudes of particular people. While this fact is not to be denied, it is our feeling that a far more common experience, and one that is far more serious in its negative effects on human beings, is the experience of discrimination that stems from *unconscious* biased feelings or assumptions. This includes the subtle behaviors about which the person is no longer aware as well as the unconscious incorporation of biased assumptions within the structural processes and procedures of an organization. As we have said, all rational constructions contain their underlying emotional thrust.

The notion that emotions play such a central part in our supposedly rational behavior is a very difficult idea for Americans to accept. Even if we do agree with this notion, it is still difficult to appreciate the important concerns reflected in the specific goals of an individual. This is true because those concerns are related to that person's unique social experience and it is impossible for one person to completely share the experience of another (Laing, 1967). When we say to someone, "Do you understand how I feel?", we are not asking a simple question. To understand how a person feels, you must have had the type of experience(s) that will enable you to relate to the emotional concerns that lay beneath and are reflected in the question. Intellectual understanding is not enough because the issue is not located within the intellectual realm.

Even when the question does lay within the intellectual realm such as the question, "Do you agree with this approach to the problem?", we cannot avoid the emotional concerns of both individuals that underlay the answer. Emotional concerns are the real issues in most cases of human interaction. This is why a person must be concerned with protection as he or she goes about the process of assimilating into any organization.

Dealing with "Hierarchicalism" and the Other "isms" of Organizational Life

One important implication that is readily drawn from the perspective in defining the character of organizations is that they are very political. Thus, most of the people working within organizations experience themselves as relatively powerless in the sense that they are not the ones who set the direction of the organization. Yet it is this direction that shapes and largely controls their behavior. Consequently, many employees are continually frustrated because of a perceived inability to develop creative ways to pull themselves out of the disadvantageous positions they often find themselves. Therefore, a fundamental issue facing most people in organizations is the need to find ways to acquire potency and a sense of power for themselves. Personal feelings of potency and effectiveness are basic ingredients that enable people to make more productive contributions to their organizations. Yet, even as we say this, we are aware of a major obstacle in this argument.

If, indeed, a basic need of individuals in organizations is the acquisitions of power so that they can feel effective and influential, a major problem is how to gain that power without disrupting the important social relationships that hold the system together. We know that organizations are means for providing individual and collective ends. Human beings, who have limited capacities, need to combine their limited actions with the limited actions of others in order to gain a certain amount of mastery over the environment. Thus, the members of any organization are "inescapably interdependent" with the other members of the organization. This is very important. The interdependence, which connects members of an organization together, makes unrealistic polarization very destructive to the effectiveness of collective goal achievement.

This is a real dilemma. When a person experiences the negative effects of "hierarchicalism" or "elitism" or any one of the other "isms" which tend to dehumanize, the last thing that is on their minds is the importance of maintaining the social relationships which are necessary to promote the organization. The natural reaction is to want to strike back, to hurt as badly as one is experiencing him or herself being hurt. And, the object of this aggression is usually other members of the organization who are seen as the culprits or the instigators of the pain. We forget that we are part of a social organization that has a definite purpose. We also forget that, to achieve those purposes, the organizations must exercise control over behaviors that are in conflict with its objectives. This must be done irrespective of the fact that most people resent having their behavior altered. How do we get out of the dilemma in such a situation?

We can get one answer to this problem from looking at the example of people who manage to have a positive outlook on life's events regardless of the devastation that is being created around them and the attack that is being directed against them. The biblical example of Job is one such case. We can also call to mind numerous examples of people who have endured horrendous attacks upon their physical and psychological well being, yet they remain positive, optimistic and steadfast in their commitment to "overcome" and progress. What keeps these people moving forward and positive? Some may say it is their faith, others have other answers. Whatever is occurring, one thing is very clear. These individuals do not spend their time identifying culprits and blaming them for their problems.

Basically, what this suggests is that the way to work effectively through the kinds of dilemmas created by organizational life is for the individual to somehow get beyond "blaming." That is, the person must get beyond the trap of spending his or her time identifying culprits and trying to make them pay for what they have done. The attitude that we wish to convey is described very well by Nancy Friday in her book *My Mother / My Self* (pp. 83-84). It is at the very end of her second chapter entitled "A Time to be Close." The statement comes after a very effective description of the power and pain associated with mother/daughter symbiosis:

> *In the name of fairness, and reality too, let me add an important postscript which is true not only for this chapter but of this whole book: Looking over our shoulder at what mother may or may not have done so many years ago locks us into the past. 'She did it. There is nothing I can do about it.'* ***Blaming mother*** *keeps us passive, tied to her. It helps us avoid taking responsibility for ourselves.*

The same point is true for anyone who chooses to concentrate too much of their time and energy focusing on what is considered to be previous injustices. No one can deny the fact that injustices occur in this society and they occur in our organizations. Some of these injustices have a profoundly damaging effect on the motivation, spirit and development of the individuals who are subjected to them. However, Ms. Friday's point still holds. Blaming the past helps us avoid taking responsibility for ourselves and the situation in which we find ourselves and this is the real issue for the future development of the person, the organization or a community.[43] Now, how do we do this?

Moving from a position where a person uses anger and blaming as the major response to adversity to a position where he or she starts to take responsibility for themselves requires difficult preparatory work. The person is leaving the dependent, childlike world of the reasonably secure direction that comes from others. Taking responsibility for yourself means creating your own worldview and running the risk that others will not agree with you. It means a lot of thought about who and what you are, what you want, and a lot of hard work devising the strategies and tactics that will gain these things. However, above all, it means being willing to take this type of positive action with the full knowledge that you might fail and that you will bear the major responsibility for any failure.

The reader may object to our placing such a heavy burden of responsibility upon the average employee (or citizen). Isn't much of this the responsibility of management? Isn't it the manager's job to ensure that the work environment is a secure, healthy place for employees to work? Generally, we would not disagree with the logic behind such assessments. However, our real organizational experience tells us that managers, particularly middle level managers, are struggling with the same forces in organizations that are acting to dehumanize us all. As human beings, managers are also seeking a sense of significance and a way to be potent in organizations. All too often this need is satisfied by building and flaunting certain symbols of power which act to further diminish the feelings of importance of others in the organization.

The basic fact is that organizations are complex configurations of social relationships between people who have come together to achieve some basic objectives. The organization is only as good as the "character" of these relationships. Everyone in the organization has a part in constructing the relationships and we believe that they also have an obligation to take the responsibility for ensuring that the relationships posses the kind of quality that will enhance the life of the organization. The principles which we present in the following sections are intended to help each person in the organization develop the type of perspective that will allow them to contribute significantly to the development of the system. The principles will also help to provide them with a sense of potency as they go about their work.

The Primary Principle

When a person in an organization begins to move toward a position of taking responsibility for the situations they encounter, the individual will experience the need for an orienting conceptual view, new strategies and different tactics. However, we believe one point is essential to success. The individual will need to find ways to address "reality" more often than what he or she would "like reality to be." To this end, we have devised a simple tactical principle:

> *We must "know" and "realistically accept" what is. "Accept" in this context does not mean necessarily that we must agree with what happens to be. It means that we must recognize and listen to what our intellect and our senses tell us about the reality of the organizational environment.*

We have said that organizations are means to specific human ends. All organizations have a basic purpose for existing (the instrumental rationality). They have technology and people who use the available technology to accomplish the tasks of the organization. Finally, all organizations have various types of control mechanisms that help to keep in on course. These main components of an organization constantly interact to create the organization's culture. This is the essence of the organization and this is what we must discern, know and accept about the organizations we experience. The natural tendency is to view this reality as positive or negative based upon the way we personally experience it but that type of stance gets in the way of what we are proposing. Again, this is the organization's culture and it is no one's fault. It simply *is* what it *is*. We must respect it and understand it in order to protect ourselves if this is necessary and we must also respect and understand it if we are to act effectively to change it for the better.

Figure 3 illustrates our conception of how the culture, more specifically, *the socio-technical culture* of an organization is formed. Every work organization is composed of both social and technical components as factors. The number, kind and arrangement of the organization's social factors (its people) interact over time to form the *social context* of the organization. Similarly, the particular nature, arrangement and utilization of the technical factors combine to form the organization's *technical context.*

It is the constant and dynamic interaction among the components that comprise the social context and those that comprise the technical context that create the particular socio-technical culture of the organization. Thus, the socio-technical culture is a reality that emerges from a specific socio-technical situation. Its "character" depends on the particular individuals involved in the system, the tasks they have to perform, the structures that are established to help them do their work, the social controls that are operative and the kinds of experiences they have shared throughout their history.

One important implication from Figure 3 is that the socio-technical culture is a "logical" reality that stems from the historical interactions of the key components of the organization. When seen in this way there is no mystery about its creation. Also, there is no mistaking the fact that the socio-technical culture can be changed over time by planned change in the two major components that work together to create it. Making change in a social system is a complex, difficult business that requires time and concentrated energy devoted to analysis and specific tactical action. However, the individual can use the same knowledge of culture development to manage his or her entry into the culture and to control in some ways their experience in the system.

Figure 3
DEVELOPMENT OF THE SOCIO-TECHNICAL CULTURE

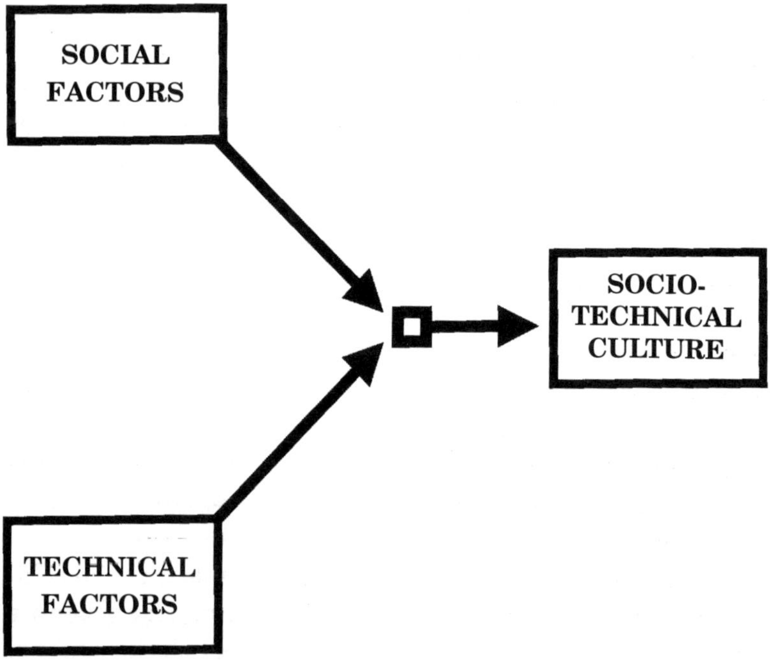

Analysis: The Pre-work to Tactical Action

When a person finds himself in a social system that doesn't seem to quite mesh with who and what he is, he must take action to protect himself. This action must be specific, it must be analytical and it must be tactical. Taking tactical action gives the person the sense of being proactive about events experienced and it requires a broader kind of perspective that will help the person see a bigger picture. In this way the individual can more effectively address the problems being experienced without the negative drain on energy and outlook that comes from emotional reactions to events.

There are a number of steps in the analytical process that prepares a person for tactical action in a social system. The first step requires the person to spend time observing and understanding the components which give rise to, maintain and add substance to what is the current cultural reality of the system. We know from Figure 3 that the cultural reality is a product of the technology and the people in the system interacting together over time. Therefore, to understand what is being experienced, the person must understand the technical and social inputs to the situation.

For example, the technical input includes such things as the hierarchical structure defining who is in relationship with whom and who is dominant in the relationship; it includes the actual physical structure of the work place as well as the equipment being used. These structures place various kinds of limits on the activities that can occur in the work place and sometimes they place a strain on the humans who must work under these conditions. The technology also includes such items as the formal rules and procedures that are established to control the work. These technical factors all affect the people in the system and reaction to them can be observed directly.

The social inputs are the individual people and the relationships that have been established over time. By listening to and observing the behavior of individuals in the system, we can learn a great deal about the character of the social culture. We can learn how important information is communicated to people; we can learn who are the true leaders of opinion or the philosophy of the unit. It should always be remembered that philosophy usually precedes and directs actions. However, philosophy is both articulated and acted out so if we are to trust what we are learning, we have to listen and observe. People do tend to act out of what they believe, especially when they are off front stage and on their own time.

From careful observation and thought about the technical and social inputs to a system, the individual can get a very good idea of the nature of the system. The person should have an idea of the kinds of expectations that exist in the system both in terms of task performance and social behavior. Additionally, there will be solid information available concerning the expected response to direction from the hierarchy. Whatever conclusion is derived from this analysis, it is important to refrain from allowing your particular values to interfere with the understanding of what exists. The cleaner the description of "what is," the more useful it will be in the development of tactical actions.

A second step in the process leading toward tactical action, if it has not been completed before, is for the individual to analyze and "really know" him or herself. By this we mean that the person must be willing to accept all that he or she knows or has learned about him or herself even though some of the things may not be very pleasant. For example, a person may not like the effect they observe on fellow employees when another person uses their authority but they know from past experience that they like to be in control and to use authority to get things done. It is important to accept the latter bit of data about one's self. Such a bank of knowledge will enable the person to become sensitive to and to identify those places in the organization where he or she is a "realistic misfit."

This is a very crucial point. The difference between the

cultural reality or social requirement of a system and the natural assets a person obtains from their own primary and secondary socialization is their perceived deviance. People will make assessments of the person's productive worth based on the perceived match between the system's priorities and his or her assets. Another way of saying the same thing is that the difference between these two realities will represent the person's "predictable powerlessness." It is predictable because influence is a function of a person's fit to the requirements of an organization. Misfit produces reservations and suspicion.

When, however, the person understands the perception which others have of them based upon their "fit" with the important values of the system, there is a choice to make. Either the person can attempt to draw him or herself closer to the system by assimilating its values or they can try to change those values or they could leave the organization physically or otherwise opt out. The major point here is that the person has a choice and it is he or she who controls the directions of their experience through that choice.

If the person decides to act, then it is a matter of clarifying what it is that he or she wants to do, analyzing what is required to pull it off and coming to a reasonable conclusion about the best way to go about it. Figure 4 is a useful scheme that illustrates the kind of thought processes and actions that will be required by the person in order to act effectively in a "hostile" social culture. Hostile may seem like a harsh word to use but it is accurate, given the particular situation we are describing. Every day the spirit, hope, drive and career potential of Black people are smothered to death under a blanket of deeply imbedded, institutionalized racism and anti Black deficit philosophy. Sometimes, the situation leads to events that cause actual physical death.

When a person is immersed in a culture that doesn't fit who he or she is, there is a little chance of drawing from that culture the kind of human support and psychological nour-

Figure 4

STRATEGY FOR MANEUVERING IN HOSTILE CULTURES

List of Personal Characteristics	→	List of Likely Reactions	→	Strength and Reality Testing Strategies	→	Disconfirmation or Balancing Strategies
—Handicapped Person —Jewish Person —Female Person —Elderly Person **—Black Person** —Ugly Person —Weak Build —Muscular Build		Sensitive about my feelings on race Uneasy in my presence Believe that I cannot be objective on Black issues Suspicious of conversations in private with females Doubtful of skill or professional competence		The general idea is to test the depth, strength or truth of a particular reaction by acting in a way that is likely to confirm the belief if it exist. Activity such as rumors or increased resistance will signal where some of the problem cases are in the organization. These data need to be noted but not acted upon. The objective is to simply document where problems may exist.		Once certain areas of misconception in the system have been identified, you should begin to modify your overt behavior at variance with the known stereotype in small consistent degrees. This change begins to give the impression that you are seeing the error of your ways and changing your behavior accordingly. Altering behavior in small consistent ways is important because it is closer to real change.

ishment a person needs to maintain a strong sense of themselves and their capabilities. Human beings need the psychological stimulation that comes from positive social acceptance almost as badly as they need actual physical stimulation. Such stimulation (psychological and physical) is necessary for the person to elaborate him or herself and to grow. The absence of it is really detrimental and hostile.

The *process* illustrated in Figure 4 is the important point. It helps the person take appropriate action in hostile environments so that they can obtain some of the stimulation they need. The process begins with a list of personal characteristics. This is a general list set up for the purpose of illustrating the ideas. The actual physical characteristics of a person will evoke certain responses from people in a social environment long before the person has had any opportunity for a deeper expression of him or herself. Even after the person has had opportunity to relate more deeply with others, their specific physical characteristic will continue to shape the nature of some of the response.

For example, if a person is handicapped (a paraplegic, let us say) they can expect certain kinds of reactions from non-handicapped individuals. Much of this behavior is predictable due to the patterns that have been set from countless repetitions of the experience in past social situations. The patterns form social rituals that are like scripts in a play (Goffman). Each participant seems to play his or her part as if there is an invisible director calling the shots and controlling the action. It is, however, this predictability that allows the individual the opportunity to affect the outcome of the situation. It allows the individual the chance to act out of the script and thereby create a little surprise that opens the way for him or her to build a more rewarding connection to the people in the social situation. The process in Figure 4 illustrates one possible track that could be taken using one of the most dominant personal characteristics in American Society — that of being Black.

When a Black person enters a social situation that is not predominantly Black, there is a wide range of behavioral reaction he or she could reasonably expect. People may be uncertain of how to talk to the person because they will not be aware of how sensitive he or she may be about their Blackness. If the Black person is male, there may be suspicion and competition with regard to his relationship with available females. Historically, Black people have had to experience some very hard times, and there is a need to gain power so they can feel effective and influential. However, a major problerm is how to gain that power without disrupting vital social relationships and making the problem worse. The important point here is to realize that whatever is listed as a likely reaction to a physical characteristic, the items represent only stereotypic possibilities that exist given social history. In other words, they are the stereotypes that the person carries in their head based on their past experience (personal and associative). Sometimes people act on these expectations as if they are reality and create more chaos than existed originally.

Once the person has generated a list of the likely responses from people in a social situation he or she, then, needs to do some testing. The testing is simple but it is important for two basic reasons. One is that the test is necessary to identify where the real pockets of resistance and negative feeling exist. It is also necessary because some of the expectations will be disconfirmed and this will help the person develop by refining, changing or letting go of stereotypes that are no longer relevant to the situations he or she encounters.

To test *likely reactions,* all the person has to do is behave in a way that confirms the stereotype that is associated with the reactions. As we have said already, these situations are like scripts in a play. If a person is playing the part of a bigot or if they actually are in reality, the behavior in reaction to a Black person "getting out of their place" will be predictable.

The actor at this point is doing just that. He or she is acting a part and collecting data concerning the response that is received. This data collection process will eventuate in the individual having a better, more realistic, assessment of his or her social position and the possibilities that are available. The person will also be able to more specifically identify who, what and where the real problem exists.

Now, the second part of the action comes into play. Once certain areas of misconception in the system are identified, the person should begin to modify his or her overt behavior at variance with the associated stereotype in small consistent degrees. It is necessary to vary behavior in small degrees because the behavior must be believable in order to tap into existing stereotypes. Behavior too far outside that expected from the stereotypes will alert the other actors that something is definitely wrong and will elicit a mustering of their counter defenses. By altering social behavior in small degrees, the person is, in effect, changing the script, he or she is not playing their part like they are supposed to and it tends to create questions. "Why are they not behaving like they are supposed to?" This is the small opening that the individual needs to present himself more realistically to the significant people in the system. It is his chance to act in a way that will give him a small degree of influence in the social system. Creating and taking such opening is one effective way for individuals in hostile cultures to maintain a sense of proactivity and potency.

Now, before we proceed further, a word of warning to the wise. Whether or not a person sets down and actually spells out a model like that in Figure 4, most human beings use such tactics. We use them in all kinds of social situations to help us achieve a wide range of social objectives anywhere from picking up a date for an evening to landing a choice job. However, one must never fall into the trap of believing that such analyses do anything more than generate a few plausible hypotheses that can be systematically tested out to help direct the person's actions. A second caveat is that the person using the approach must be sure of the quality of his or her end goals. Failure to do this may mean that feelings of manipulation will seriously threaten the consistency and congruence in verbal and non-verbal behavior that is so vital to success.

Tactical Action

With the decision to act and an idea of how to proceed, the person is not ready for the creation or the specific "means" or tactics for implementing his or her desires. It is at this stage where the personal values must be brought back into the picture and used to condition the choices of action. Effective action requires integrity to be sustained so it is crucial that the person not engage in behavior that violates fundamental values that he or she holds. If we fail to adhere to this basic point, the actions simply will not be very effective. At times this will be a very difficult principle to follow because a person's values will not always support the actions which the analysis suggests is most appropriate for the particular situation. Still, acting incongruent with deeply held values is ineffective and weak. Below are four important considerations related to successful tactical action.

(1) When anyone engages in the process of tactic implementation, he or she must accept the fact that they are entering into a "power game." It doesn't have to be a very serious power game but it is a game nonetheless and you must realize that you share an equal part of the responsibility for its creation and the repercussions which stem from it. Moral rationalizations or expressions of benign intentions are irrelevant behaviors because once power forces are released by a tactic, it will be responded to positively or negatively regardless of the initiator's specific intent. THE

CRUCIAL POINT AT THIS STAGE OF THE PROCESS FOR THE PERSON SEEKING POWER IS THAT HE OR SHE CRITICALLY ASSESS AND DEFINE FOR THEMSELVES WHAT IT MEANS TO "WIN." Without such an assessment *a priori,* the person will not be able to get a sense of directed progress toward the objective. The person will also be less able to understand and control the natural expansive nature of all power games.

(2) There are many forms of power. Everyone has some form of power which they control and are able to use for their benefit. The person seeking more influence must have a good sense of which forms of power he or she controls and which ones they do not; he or she must know which forms will aid and which ones, for particular reasons or circumstances will not be helpful. Every power form has a source and certain situational limitations. In other words, in the natural course of a power game, you must be able to discern when it is time to "eat crow." It is our belief that you must learn how to enjoy these periods as if you were dining on a rare delicacy.

(3) A person acquiring new forms of power or using his or her resources to gain access to other areas has to keep in mind where "home base" is located. This is the place where the person has the birth right of unconditional support. It is the place where the person can rest and regroup; a place where the tactical defenses so necessary in the power game can be relaxed. It is important to keep this home base in mind because, as the person moves out into other power arenas, there is the

possibility that he or she may be forced to engage in some behaviors that will be experienced by members of the home base support group as in violation of some basic values. This will tend to have an effect similar to that of "burning the bridges behind an advancing army." If this in fact happens, the person is really in trouble in the balance of the power game. Cut off the source of rest and recuperation and strength, the person will be worn down and defeated in the same way that an army cut off from the support of its home base is worn down.

(4) The final consideration in tactical action is an identification of the specific resources a person has at his or her command and to come to a determination of how to best deploy these resources for the greatest effect. Whatever direction a person chooses to focus the resources under his control, it is key that they be arranged so that they are used to achieve a very specific goal which relates to another specific goal at a higher level and so on. This type of tactical structure will widen the person's perspective into an overall strategy and will provide him or her with the sense of controlled progress. Under this system, any tactic that fails to achieve its objective will be viewed as losing only one of the battles in the war and not the whole war.

---

[43] The community perspective was added recently because of the author's current work as a community development consultant for the depressed inner city community of College Hill in North St. Louis.

<u>Appendix 3</u>

HONOR THY FATHER AND THY MOTHER BUT KILL WILLIELYNTOLOGY

By
Howard Bowens, Ph.D.

HONOR THY FATHER AND THY MOTHER BUT KILL WILLIELYNTOLOGY

In Exodus 20:12 the Lord says to, *"Honour thy father and thy mother: that thy days may be long upon the land which the Lord thy God giveth thee."* This commandment is one of the vital principles which help ensure family stability and community development. In this paper I recommend a selective violation of this honored commandment. My recommendation is that we (all African-American people who are descendants from former slaves) conscientiously and systematically "kill" one of our possible forefathers, "Daddy" Willie Lynch.

"Daddy" Lynch was a person who wanted African-American people to forever remain slaves, little children who would passively submit to the abusive exploitation which supported and still supports the personal gratification of his favored race. Throughout this article I refer to Willie Lynch as *"Daddy."* The reference will always be in quotations. The quotations denote first a dripping sarcasm that I trust will be obvious. Secondly, the quotations denote the possibility that the reference could be a distinct historical fact. Given the system that Willie proposed for the control of slaves, I have little doubt that he took every opportunity and great pleasure in personally "fathering" through rape a host of illegitimate offspring to use as fuel for his insidious, but effective, strategy. Who was Big "Daddy" Willie Lynch?

"Daddy" Lynch was an 18th Century British slaveowner who authored a system of mind control designed to lock African-American people forever out of our God given right to develop into strong, mature, interdependent and responsible adults. The story of Willic Lynch is told in chilling detail by Mr. George Fraser in his new book *Success Runs in Our Race* (pp. 65-67). The entire section on Willie is quoted below for your convenience. Read it slowly and carefully. This is the scientific system of mind control that has wreaked such havoc on our ability to prosper through collective action. I refer to it as the "Science of Willielyntology."

The Enemy Within

(excerpted from Mr. George Fraser's *Success Runs in Our Race)*

While there are racial and societal forces at work on us from the outside, a certain portion of our problem lies within. From the days of our enslavement, many of us bought into the slave mentality. We accepted the white man's pronouncement that we were an inferior race, and even when we came to understand that it was a false pronouncement, it continued to dominate our collective psyches; it was a powerful indoctrination.

The following is an infamous and chilling example of how that mentality was ingrained into our ancestors, and into succeeding generations. It is taken from a speech given by Willie Lynch, from whose name the term lynching is derived. Lynch was a British slave owner in the West Indies, probably of Jamaican heritage, who used mind-control techniques on his black slaves and then advocated the use of those manipulative techniques to other slave owners. He was invited to the colony of Virginia in 1712 to teach his methods to slave owners there, and these are his words as passed down. I think you will find them haunting:

> *Gentlemen: I greet you here on the bank of the James River in the year of Our Lord one thousand seven hundred and twelve. First, I shall thank you The Gentlemen of the Colony of Virginia for bringing me here. I am here to help you solve some of your problems with slaves. Your invitation reached me on my modest plantation in the West Indies where I have experimented with some of the newest and still oldest*

methods for control of slaves. Ancient Rome would envy us if my program is implemented. As our boat sailed south on the James River, named for our illustrious King, whose version of the Bible we cherish, I saw enough to know that your problem is not unique. While Rome used cords of wood as crosses for standing human bodies along its old highways in great numbers, you are here using the tree and the rope on occasion.

I caught the whiff of a dead slave hanging from a tree a couple miles back. You are not only losing valuable stock by hangings, you are having uprisings, slaves are running away, your crops are sometimes left in the field too long for maximum profit, you suffer occasional fires, your animals are killed, gentlemen, you know what your problems are; I do not need to elaborate. I am not here to enumerate your problems, I am here to introduce you to a method of solving them.

In my bag here, I have a fool proof method of controlling Black Slaves. I guarantee everyone of you that if installed correctly, it will control the slaves for at least 300 years. My method is simple and members of your family and any Overseer can use it.

I have outlined a number of difference(s) among the slaves; and I take these differences and make them bigger. I use fear, distrust, and envy for control purposes. These methods have worked on my modest plantation in the West Indies and [they] will work throughout the South. Take this simple little list of differences, think about them. On top of my list is "Age" but it is there only because it begins with "A." The second is "Color" or "Shade," there is intelligence, size, sex, size of plantation, status of plantation, attitude of owner, whether the slaves live in the valley, on a hill, East, West, North, or South, have a fine or coarse hair, or is tall or short. Now that you have a list of differences, I shall give you an outline of action but before that, I shall assure you that distrust is stronger than trust and envy is stronger than adulation, respect and admiration.

The Black Slave, after receiving this indoctrination, shall carry on and will become self-refueling and self-generating for hundreds of years, maybe thousands.

Don't forget you must pitch the old black versus the young black and the young black male against the old black male. You must use the dark skin slave vs. the light skin slaves and the light skin slaves vs. the dark skin slaves. You must also have your white servants and overseers distrust all blacks, but it is necessary that your slaves trust and depend on us. They must love, respect and trust only us.

Gentlemen, these Kits are keys to control, use them. Have your wives and children use them, never miss an opportunity. My plan is guaranteed and the good thing about this plan is that if used intensely for one year the slaves themselves will remain perpetually distrustful.

Thank you, gentlemen.

Each time I read "Daddy" Willie's words, I shudder. He was a diabolical genius. If you are an African-American descendant from this slave legacy, whether a member of the wealthy elite or the embodiment of the so called "underclass" and, if you are honest with yourself, you know that our people have been honoring "Daddy" Lynch's system most of our natural lives. Willie confidently declared in his lecture in 1712 that if his plan was "used intensely for one year, the slaves themselves will remain perpetually distrustful." Willie also offered a guarantee. He promised his slave-owning audience that *"if installed correctly"* it would control the slaves for *"at least 300 years."*

In six years, "Daddy" Willie Lynch will have made good on his minimum guarantee. I acknowledge the possibility of a relationship to this "bastard maker." I also acknowledge the effectiveness and resilience of his system. But, I am intelligent enough to know that "any" control system, correctly installed or not can be disassembled. The process for accomplishing this is detailed in the conclusion of this article. It is based upon the same true psychological principles which are the foundation of "Daddy" Lynch's system. Like "Daddy" Lynch, I can confidently guarantee that if we institute these simple "deprogramming techniques" over the course of the next ten years, we will *MAKE BIG "DADDY" LYNCH A LIE.* The objective is to kill "Willielyntology" before "Daddy" Lynch rolls over in his grave in the year 2012 and smugly says, "See, I told you it would work."

Before I lay out the system for dismantling the destructive effects of "Willielyntology," there is one very important aspect of "Daddy" Lynch's system that must be understood. It is a key reason for its enormous success. This vital aspect is its *simplicity.* It was simple, concise, easy to implement and easy to teach. It didn't require massive outlays of capital or huge bureaucratic administrative structures. This point is absolutely essential because the only effective remedy is one that is likewise simple, concise, easy to do or implement and easy to pass on to our family, friends and children.

We need no new national organizations; we need no big meetings or strategy conferences. We need only recognize and honestly acknowledge what has been done to us as a people to destroy our capability for sustained progressive collective action. Lynch's system attacked our *ability to trust one another,* the core social ingredient which enables people to *work together for a common goal.*

While the system offered below is simple, it will still not be easy for us to do. For generations we have believed and honored the notions which underlay "Daddy" Lynch's system. Rather than focus on the mind control system as a major cause of underproductivity, we have continuously used notions of inherent inferiority to explain away or justify our lack of collective achievement. We have often acted, as Lynch said we would, in ways that "refuel" the very system that controls us. No, it won't be easy to follow my recommendations for change. It won't be easy to "dishonor" our "daddy" Willie but that is exactly what we have to do to make him a lie. Now, what do I recommend that we do? Simply stated, I recommend that we each undergo a "Willielynchectomy."

Steps in the "Willielynchetomy"

Step 1: Buy Mr. George Fraser's book, *Success Runs in Our Race. BUY IT!* Why? There are two reasons. First, Black people can and do afford almost everything they really want. Buying the book is a direct behavioral statement that you believe in and value this opportunity. I believe the Virginia slave owners who heard Willie Lynch speak in 1772 demonstrated their belief in his system by *purchasing* the "kits" that he said were the answer to their problems. Second, the book offers a comprehensive philosophy and sound action techniques for implementing African-American economic development through the universal principles of effective networking and teamwork.

Step 2: Copy Willie Lynch's strategy from Mr. Fraser's book (pp. 65-67). I have also separated the speech at the end of this paper for this purpose. Place the speech in several strategic locations in your home:

- The kitchen refrigerator door.
- The wall directly opposite the toilet seat.
- The wall just behind and above the family television set.

- If you are really bold, tape it to the outside of your front door.

Step 3: Read Lynch's remarks to the slaveowners at least once a day, *EVERY DAY.*

Step 4: I said in the body of the paper that we should "dishonor" Daddy Lynch. That is not completely correct. Step four is the critical action component of the "Willielynchectomy." *Honor or do everything that Willie Lynch outlines but DO IT IN REVERSE!* Where he says to maximize the differences between you and other brothers and sisters, *minimize* those insignificant differences. When he tells you to hate and distrust all Black people, extend to them *unconditional love and trust* even if, NO, *especially if it is not earned.* Finally, where he says that you are to love, respect and trust only his kind, *require only his kind* to *earn* your love, respect and trust.

Step 5: Commit yourself to follow this system for the next ten to seventeen years. In 18 years from now Willie Lynch's initial promise to his audience will have been fulfilled. If we fail to make him a lie by that time, recommit yourself so that his insidious system doesn't stand for a thousand years.

Step 6: Challenge the powerful little Willie Lynch voice that is now telling you that none of this will really work. Willie Lynch is depending upon your resistance to my plan because he knows that his system is safe as long as we stay in denial about our brainwashing and as long as we continue to refuse to actively reverse the negative conditioning that his system so expertly applied to our "collective psyches."

Conclusion

Dr. Martin Luther King once gave a great speech about his "dream." When I was in the process of writing this paper,

I paused one moment and began to "daydream." I think I would like to do some research and locate the grave site of Big "Daddy" Willie Lynch. In the year 2012, I would like to show up at his grave site with close friends. The purpose of the visit will be to place one of two possible posters. If we have been successful with our "Willielynchectomy," the sign will read something like "THERE, TAKE THAT, YOU BASTARD MAKER." If we have not been successful, the sign will read "OKAY, BASTARD MAKER, YOU WON THE 300 YEAR SKIRMISH BUT THIS IS A THOUSAND YEAR WAR. SEE YOU IN 2712."

Appendix 4

STEMMING THE TIDE OF BLACK PROFESSIONAL SUICIDE: A CALL FOR POINT PEOPLE

By
Howard Bowens, Ph.D.

STEMMING THE TIDE OF BLACK PROFESSIONAL SUICIDE: A CALL FOR POINT PEOPLE

Justin Evan Collier had most of the middle class accouterments that we aspire to — an Ivy League education, a good position in a Fortune 500 Company, leadership roles in the "correct" community groups. Bernita, Justin's wife, was a bright and extremely attractive woman who was decisively moving up within her own professional arena. Their choice of a home on Cleveland's Gold Coast was certainly atypical, since few Blacks of any social class lived west of the Cuyahoga River. Nonetheless, this seemed to solidify their position near the top of the Black professional class. Justin and Benita had a few more children than most — his, hers and theirs. They ranged from a two-year-old girl to twin college-aged sons. Everything seemed as perfect as one could hope for until Justin walked into a wholly white neighborhood bank and announced his intention to rob it or blow it up. He then sat and waited while bank employees hurriedly collected the money and pressed the silent alarm. Justin, money and fake bomb in tow, walked out to his car and attempted to drive away. His efforts to leave were thwarted by the suburban policemen who shot him repeatedly as he sat in his car. They said that Justin attempted to run them over with his car and that their actions were clearly self defense. Paralyzed from the neck down, Justin languished and died two months later.

This is how Jacquie McLemore-Jackson begins her gripping paper, "Culture Double Binds: Some Propositions." Ms. McLemore writes an extremely powerful piece describing the kind of cultural bind that many Black professionals find themselves confronting as they attempt, as Black people, to pursue their share of the "Great American Dream." It is a bind that strikes the Black professional at a time-of-life crisis and drives many to a variety of types of suicide. Justin Collier committed suicide.

There are a lot of potential Justins out there, myself included, and we know what it is to feel the twists and pulls created by our living in dual cultures. We know what it is to be in Justin's predicament even though we have made different decisions in attempting to resolve the dissonance that we feel. However, we still need help and we need to help each other because this situation (the cultural double bind) is no minor problem for Black professionals.

The Black professional, reared in one culture with its own norms, goals, customs and constraints, is faced in corporate life with the problems of socialization into the mainstream of another culture. The turmoil seems to be created by the need to make continuous "bipolar choices." Should the Black professional hang on to and affirm the cultural elements of the culture of origin? Would he or she be allowed to do this even if this option were chosen? Should the Black professional, on the other hand, submit to the resocialization forces and be partly assimilated into the dominant culture? Will he or she be allowed to do this? Beal and Kennedy, in their book *Corporate Cultures,* which we will discuss later, suggest that this may be a problem.

In further substantiating her case, Ms. McLemore recounts the story of William Brock, another Black manager in yet another big corporate organization and, yes, another Black suicide. Appearing in the news article concerning the tragic suicide of Mr. Brock were two assessments of the situation. Both seem very consistent with our argument about the drastic effects of the culture double bind. Jeffrey Speller, a psychiatrist, said, "You're caught in two worlds. You're black, trying to survive in two cultures ... you get depressed and frustrated ... you feel polarized and isolated." Then a Justice named Dennis Schatzman made this assessment, "This is the classic dilemma of the black man in the corporate world. You're in the position of asking yourself, am I going to defend the corporation or am I going to join my people? Where do my loyalties lie?"

Before we rush in too quickly with an answer to Mr. Schatzman's questions, here is what two top consultants (Deal and Kennedy) say in their excellent book, *Corporate Cultures* (pp. 78-82):

> *Day-to-day life in a company's culture revolves around countless repetitions of unwritten but well-understood rituals. Mostly social in context, one purpose they serve among others is to initiate newcomers to the culture. When the newcomer is different — a woman in a man's world, or a black in a white managerial echelon — no rituals exist to socialize this individual. In the place of comfortable rituals are taboos: "Don't hustle that woman;" or "Blacks are sensitive, so be careful not to hurt their feelings."*

Do we need any more confirmation of the ominous position Black professionals are faced with in the white corporate world. We believe the references above adequately portray the problem and the constant threat to the mental health and professional success of Black managers. But, what is the answer?

Ms. McLemore suggests that one answer lies in the Black professional's ability to choose between what critic Elenor Traylor refers to as "sensibilities" or "ways of being in the world." The individual must choose because the belief and value systems from the two cultures are constantly at odds. This experience of cultural contradiction visits the person through the specific "messages" which are received from each culture. For example, consider the list of contradictory messages from the minority and majority cultures outlined in Figure 5, and imagine the pressure on the Black professional caught between them at a time when he or she is trying to sort out their career (McLemore, p. 11):

Figure 5
MIXED MESSAGES FROM CULTURES

Minority Culture Messages		**Majority Culture Messages**
Education is the way up.	→	Some of us have it and some of us don't
Don't forget where you came from.	→	To be successful, your job has to be first.
You have a responsibility to your people	→	Don't look back. Keep looking ahead.
The system won't let you make it.	→	You're different (better) from the rest of them.

These messages, according to Ms. McLemore are "*translated into behaviors, codified into laws and designed into organizations . . . . A culture double bind may then be defined as a minority individual's experience of turmoil resulting from being faced with bipolar choices. These bipolar choices call into question explicit, implicit and intentional messages communicated from the minority culture of origin and the dominant culture. The management of the culture double bind results in either an affirmation of the minority culture of ori-*

gin through a process of secondary socialization or a displacing of the culture of origin and a resocialization to a way of being in the dominant culture." Thus, one answer is a choice between the above two sensibilities.

The choice between either of these "sensibilities" is not enough, however. The young Black professional still needs help from "guides" or "mentors" who have experienced the force of these pressures and who possess information about how to avoid the devastating impact of the bipolar choicepoint. There are no easy answers, but if we are to reduce the wasteful result represented by the cases of Justin collier and William Brock, Black professionals must use their knowledge and experience to create "ways of being" in corporate organizations that will enable the new generations of Black professionals to develop mechanisms to deal with the constant assault on their personality by a diet of bipolar choices.

This paper is, in effect, a call for a collective consciousness among Black professionals presently struggling with these forces. In a paper entitled, "Living and Growing in Hostile Cultures," this author attempted to offer another option or "sensibility" for people who find themselves in cultures that don't quite fit who and what they are. The paper was written for individuals in general under the influence of organizational forces, although the particular perspective that is taken is an outgrowth of the author's Black experience.

To live and grow in a hostile culture requires a concerted effort on the part of the individual to become aware of the important elements of the culture and to take tactical action to make a small place for him or herself in the culture. The person may never become fully integrated into the fundamental structure of the culture but he or she will have a sense of potency and control which are very important to maintaining energy and a positive sense of self.

The strategies offered in the paper are very useful in helping a person maneuver his way through the cultural pathways of the modern complex organization. However, the cultural double bind problem we have discussed in this paper is a specific difficulty for the Black professional in organizations. The Black professional not only has the difficult task of joining and performing in often foreign organizational culture, he also has to deal with the issues of affirmation, maintenance or the loss of basic elements of a Black culture from which he or she has emerged. The sense you have is that you are being asked to give up something very fundamental and important in order to succeed in the corporate world. You try to ignore it and proceed as if you can progress and maintain both cultural identities but, at times of major life changes, the two contradictory cultures present the person with incompatible choices that are extremely disorienting.

This problem has been with us a long time and it is very complex. But, in answer to one aspect of the problem, this author calls for a kind of collective consciousness and a collective responsibility from a certain group of Black professionals. They are people who, to use a military analogy, are "on the point." *Point People* are those who are experiencing the direct heat of cultural double binds but who have developed strategies or learned ways to survive with these pressures. Most Black professionals in white corporate organizations today are "on the point" so to speak, but not all of us can understand what I am saying and not everyone wants to spend his or her time being an effective person on the point. What does it mean to be an effective "person on the point."

The point person is the one who does most of the scouting work for the advancing troops. But, this person frequently doesn't get or see the benefit of his efforts. Point people take the force of the enemy head on and, by their demise, sometimes warn those who follow of the impending danger. Now, if the point person never gets back to educate the troops about the true nature and strength of the enemy, all that can be done is to continue to send out a new point person.

Black professionals in organizations have sent out a lot of point people. How much intelligent information has been collected and communicated back to the other troops about the nature, strength and location of cultural dangers so that strategic responses can be planned? I think that, for this to happen, those of us who are the new point people have to change our perspective. It is no longer satisfactory to communicate that there is cultural danger in Corporate America. Most intelligent people will know something is seriously wrong when point people don't make it through (like Justin and Brock), or when they return so battered that they only function as vegetables.

What is this new perspective? I think that we have to realize and accept the realities of the point. Our role is to first take on and experience the "fire" of the corporate culture and the binds it creates. We must gather important strategic information about this phenomena and, then, secondly, to *communicate* this information effectively to those who follow so that it can be used to secure a more stable position.

I hope that the use of this military analogy has not been distracting. It is one of the best frames of reference for describing what I see as a continuing problem — a problem that is so resilient that against all the advances that Black professionals have made in this society; in the face of all the significant contributions by talented Black people, we can still find (in 1996) the reality that Deal and Kennedy found in 1983: *"When the newcomer is different — a woman in a man's world, or a black in a white managerial echelon — no rituals exist to socialize this individual."*

This is not only sad, it is unacceptable. Those of us on the point can spend our time decrying the difficulty and thankless nature of the "point position" or we can accept the position and the challenge it represents. We can and must find a way to work together to ensure that the point experiences are successfully communicated and utilized to inform the tactical actions of others. In the wonderful words of "Trip" from the movie *Glory,* it is time to *"ante up and kick in."* Are there any "point people" out there who know what I have been talking about in this paper and who are willing to accept the challenge? I sincerely pray that there are.

<u>Appendix 5</u>

STRATEGIC COMMUNITY BUILDING: THE PROCESS OF BRINGING INTENTIONALITY AND STRATEGY INTO INNER CITY COMMUNITY DEVELOPMENT WORK

By
Howard Bowens, Ph.D.

(NOTE: This paper can be viewed as an ongoing case study application of the experiences, principles and strategies presented in the book. The paper discusses the work of one of the authors in a long-term revitalization process in the African-American community of College Hill in North St. Louis, Missouri.)

STRATEGIC COMMUNITY BUILDING: THE PROCESS OF BRINGING INTENTIONALITY AND STRATEGY INTO INNER CITY COMMUNITY DEVELOPMENT WORK

The primary purpose of this paper is to provide general information about the theory, the philosophy and the broad conceptual components that comprise a community building approach and development strategy for the revitalization of North St. Louis Neighborhoods. Why North St. Louis? I specify neighborhoods in North St. Louis because any major change process, if it is to be effective, must be relevant to the social, cultural and political realities of the environment in which it is implemented. The particular approach we are suggesting was designed for, developed and is currently being implemented in the North St. Louis Neighborhood of College Hill.

Because of and due to the specific social and political history of the State of Missouri and City of St. Louis, many of the neighborhoods north of Delmar are similar in character, demographic profile and economic status. These neighborhoods also share a common, although often unrecognized advantage with respect to development opportunity. Their advantage is that they contain the majority of the underutilized and developable land in the City of St. Louis, a city that has been land limited since 1876. Therefore, North St. Louis Communities are in a unique position in 2004 to benefit most from a strategy that could help residents organize and use the available resources to reconstruct themselves. However, in order to take advantage of this opportunity, most of these communities have to take action to rebuild vital community elements that have been allow to decay over the years.

Community Building is more than "brick and mortar." It is more than buildings, houses, streets, alleys and gangways. A real community is more than physical structure. True community is a feeling of relationship, a feeling or "sense" of being connected to other people and a sense of belonging that comes from people interacting with one another in focused, planned action. A community has a common bond, a shared interest. When attempting to rebuild a sense of community within a neighborhood that has become as disinvested as many of those in North St. Louis, a great deal of creativity has to be employed. You have to use every available avenue to provide residents with a way to "see" or experience each other as talented, resourceful human beings, as neighbors and even as friends. This "sense of community" must be built intentionally. And, it must be built upon a foundation of positive energy and tangible, sustained accomplishments.

I am what in my field is called "a change agent." By profession, I am a Senior Organization Development Consultant for Creative Marketing Consultants, Inc. based in Atlanta, Georgia. However, I was born and grew to adulthood in St. Louis. I left the city for college at eighteen and returned in my early fifties with my education complete and a lot of professional consulting experience. For the past nine years, I have been working as a volunteer consultant for the nonprofit community development organization serving the College Hill Community Neighborhood. The organization, College Hill Community 2000, Inc., has been a community based 501c(3) corporation since 1993. In the years since its birth, the organization, comprised primarily of College Hill residents, has made significant progress in implementing elements of a long-term development strategy for the entire community. This paper is modeled upon the College Hill experience. It is our intention to take lessons from that experience in order to construct a logical, practical and relevant inner city revitalization approach for other communities in North St. Louis. I refer to this approach as *Strategic Community Building*.

Community building always involves strategy. It involves planning and the implementation of plans. Therefore, in this respect, what I say in this paper is not new. It is, also, not very profound in my view except that there are some requirements for understanding what I am saying in the context of North St. Louis Communities that are not the usual expectation in community building efforts for such communities. One of the primary requirements is a willingness to look at the inner city development problem much differently than the usual "deficit model" that we have applied in the past. This requirement is not easy because many people with experience in the development industry often view the traditional processes involved in strategic planning for effective community revitalization as too complicated, too sophisticated for most inner city grass roots residents to comprehend. Therefore, the usual choice is to do much of the planning away from community residents, without much of their involvement and then bring in the plans and attempt to sell residents on their benefits. The key problem here is that it excludes these residents from participation in and learning from the very processes they will need to understand if they are to further develop and maintain their community.

Strategic Community Building, as I am using the term, is different primarily in the sense that its focus is on the concepts of "intention" and "results." Strategic Community Building is another way of saying "Intentional Community Building." What do I mean by intention?[44] In the case of the specific subset of North St. Louis Neighborhoods, Strategic Community Building means not only the intention to bring these communities back to life from decay but the intention to do it in such a way that the process protects them from continued susceptibility to the forces of that decay. This requires intense education, collaboration and involvement with the residents. It also requires that we place the focus of our intentions and our actions on the desires and the wishes of the people who are caught in, trapped by or who have self selected to be part of the communities we are trying to build. We take "their thoughts," the thoughts and wishes of the residents, and we wrap our planning expertise and development knowledge around the issues and problems they have articulated as needing resolution.[45]

Strategic Community Building as an approach begins first with a philosophical concept that is comprehensive and *non-negotiable*. The concept is that, once we have selected the boundaries that define the community we wish to build, everything that exists within that boundary or comes into it prior to the completion of the change effort is viewed as a legitimate member or stakeholder of the community. Not only is everything in the community a valid part of it but these elements need to be seriously considered with respect to all ideas and proposals for change. A second part of this philosophical concept is of equal importance. It is a commitment to the belief that the community boundaries, whatever they are specified to be, must be viewed as permeable. This is important because all boundaries defining communities or neighborhoods are artificial and often arbitrary. Boundaries need to be seen mainly as a means to help focus our energy and resources. They should not be allowed to become so rigid and fixed that they act as cement walls that exclude people or that thwart the natural human activity of relationship building and resource sharing that must occur between people, especially, those relationships that occur close to and across the artificial boundary lines.

If the comprehensive concept of community just mentioned is the first key element in Strategic Community Building, the second key element is the "process" we use to create, build and/or strengthen a "sense of community" among the residents or stakeholders inside the community boundaries we have chosen. This must be done again by intention. We intentionally build or rebuild the communications infrastructure between and among the individuals, agencies, organizations and institutions that exist within the community.

This communications infrastructure, once constructed, becomes the "social capital" building mechanism or the network that is necessary for people to effectively and meaningfully engage one another in order to create, develop and share resources. The five-step process illustrated in Figure 6 is the methodology that was used in the College Hill experience.

Healthy communities are comprised of a number of major components. The more intact and integrated these components are, the healthier and more vibrant the community. One of these major components is the communications infrastructure that we have just identified. It is this communications infrastructure and the network of organizations and cooperative systems comprising it that facilitate and allow residents to actually experience a "sense of the community." This infrastructure also provides a way for residents to construct a common community identity. Since healthy communities must possess financial, economic and political resources, this communications infrastructure also operates as the main structural mechanisms that produce and support many of the relationships that help to create these resources.

Healthy communities also have healthy physical structures. They have "brick and mortar" structures that are in good condition. These are the institutions (i.e., schools, businesses, churches and homes) from which people negotiate the daily activities of their lives. In many of the communities in North St. Louis, a great deal of this physical structure has been destroyed due to disinvestments, decay and neglect. This is true for the community of College Hill. With respect to the disinvestment problem, we often hear it said that "White Flight" was a major cause of the decline and decay. While this may appear to be a realistic and plausible explanation on the surface, it is actually very misleading and distracting. The flight of the "color white" did not cause the community decay of North St. Louis. The decay came

Figure 6
STEPS OF THE COMMUNITY BUILDING STRATEGY

When we began this effort in 1993, we knew that it would take more than our own participation. However, in the absence of any knowledge of outside resources willing to help us, we started the process on our own. The complete strategy can be laid out in the following manner:[46]

STEP 1 Identify the area.

↓

STEP 2 Physically canvass the area to identify "Anchor Families" and "Anchor Institutions." Our only definition for "Anchors" was those institutions and families who were present before the serious decline in the community and who still remain today.

↓

STEP 3 Draw up a plan to "stitch" these Anchor families and institutions together so that we can communicate a new "sense of community."

↓

STEP 4 Gradually work to improve the face of the community and to identify other families or people who can see our vision and who are willing to help.

↓

STEP 5 When we are sufficiently organized and have communicated our concept to other stakeholders and people who can help us, we will launch an effort to develop the community. This effort will have substance; comprehensive community involvement and it will be big enough to make the kind of impact that begins to create a positive momentum.

from the flight of vital financial, educational, economic and political resources. The decay came from the disinvestment of resources but we must recognize that disinvestment, whatever the rationale used for its occurrence, is a *decision* by people who are in control of investment resources. Then, and this is something that must be acknowledged, it is also important to accept the reality of America that most of the people who make these decisions about our communities are White people.

When the community building challenges in North St. Louis Neighborhoods are viewed from this economic perspective, there is a much better chance that our attention will stay focused on the real issues of resource acquisition and development and away from such erroneous issues like the color of people. As a matter of fact, what we actually discover through a consistent use of an economic perspective is that most of the resources needed to address the problems in North St. Louis Communities like College Hill are already available. The resources are available because they are brought into the St. Louis region each year from the federal government, often using the negative statistics associated with the problems plaguing these communities. There are resources for better housing, crime reduction, health care, education, youth development, job training, you name it.

The major problem is that administrators of the organizations receiving these funds often decide to divert them to other purposes or the funds are, simply, consumed by the administrative costs associated with a myriad of social programs that these organizations create believing they will ameliorate the problems. The point is that the funds are not applied to direct strategies that might eliminate the underlying structural issues that support the problem for which the resource was created. In St. Louis, we have developed and we support a lot of social programs. However, "social programs" often fail to address many of the fundamental issues that cause the social problems.

Strategic Community Building is a concept that helps us recognize this situation and provides the logical justification for a different decision. Strategic Community Building suggests that we build organizational structure and capacity within the community itself. If this capacity is within the community, if it is closer to the sources of the problems we want to solve, there is a much better chance that the resources can be applied more directly to the problems and, therefore, more efficiently and effectively. Strategic Community Building is a process that provides the community with the organizational capacity to go after or compete for the very resources that are available for the type of problems it faces. The Resource Acquisition Logic Model that is shown in Figure 7 illustrates this concept as it applies to the approach being used in the College Hill Revitalization Process. This logic model is integrated with and directly dependent upon the existence of an effective communications infrastructure which we have already said is the first step in the Strategic Community Building approach.

Finally, there is the vital issue of time. North St. Louis Communities, like College Hill, did not become the way they are instantaneously or "overnight" as we often say. The decay occurred over a long period of time and as a result of countless numbers of specific decisions regarding resource availability and the distribution of those resources.[47] In the same manner, communities like these don't get rebuilt overnight either. The process of community change takes time, a lot of time.

The time element is one of the most difficult aspects of the Strategic Community Building process to convey to residents. It is difficult because people caught in situations that have been allowed to decay to the point that they have for many North St. Louis Communities are eager to see improvement. They are very impatient. However, the difficulty with time stems not only from the nature of human impatience or "waiting for things to happen" but with the fact that many of the residents have not been part of planning processes for

Figure 7
THE RESOURCE ACQUISITION-ALLOCATION LOGIC MODEL USED BY COLLEGE HILL COMMUNITY 2000, INC. [48]

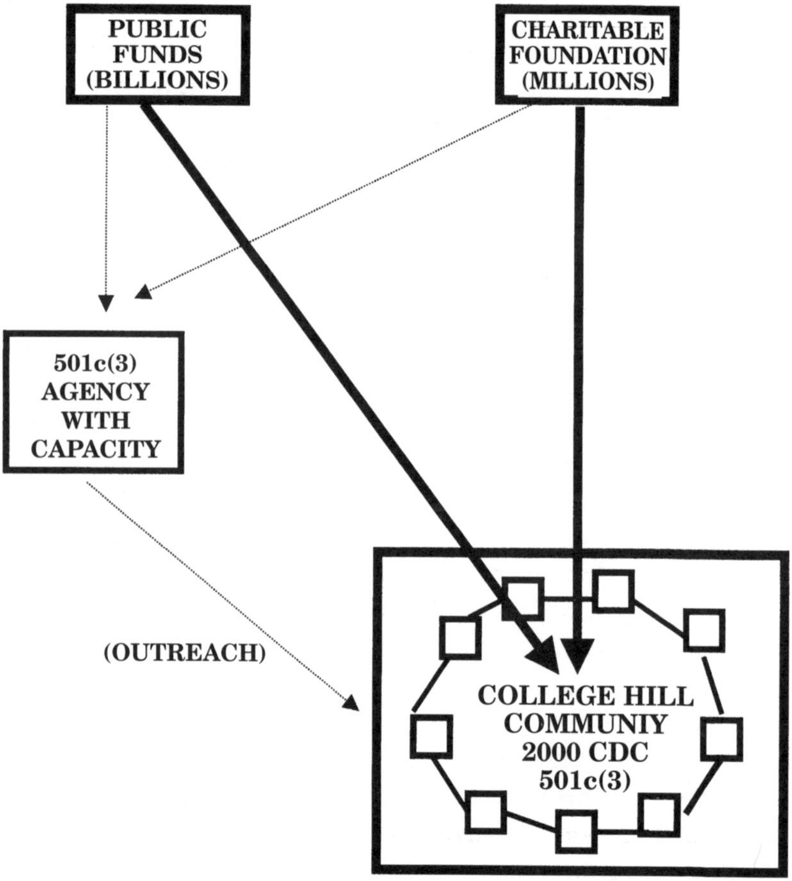

community change. Therefore, they are unfamiliar with the normal elements that make up the general "*process*" of change and with community building in particular. People, simply, don't have the experience that is required for them to understand and negotiate the various elements of the change process from where they are to where they want to be.

I once described this problem in a report to a client using the idea of "troubleshooting the middle." The example of an auto repair problem is a helpful way to convey this idea. If you are an auto mechanic, an engine breakdown is not a stressful problem because you know how to "troubleshoot the middle." You understand how an engine is designed and how it works so it is easier to get an idea of what is wrong and what will need to be done to fix the problem. If you are like me and don't possess this knowledge, the stopping of your car can cause a major trauma.

A mechanic understands the process of engine operation. He or she understands the "workings of the middle" and they often have had experience in troubleshooting engine problems. With respect to the time for repair, mechanics know that some repairs are much more difficult than others and, therefore, take more time. It is this understanding that reduces the frustration regarding time. Consequently, to reduce the frustration of inner city residents with respect to the time required for community revitalization, they must be significantly involved in the "process" of the change and continually educated about what is required in financial resources as well as energy, effort and personal determination. They also need continuous information that helps them view and properly interpret the small incremental indicators of successful change.

The model shown in Figure 8 is the way we communicate the reality of time in the College Hill Revitalization Process. Each stage was assigned an arbitrary number of seven years to be completed. In actuality, it may take us more or less time per stage. However, whatever the actual amount of time turns out to be, the important point is that this model allows us to communicate what is specifically involved in each stage and what is its outcome. We will not have completed any stage until we have achieved the clearly stated outcomes for the stage. As we make progress in and achieve the objectives within each stage, we build confidence within the residents that we will be able to achieve our ultimate objective, *the revitalization of the entire community*. We can take our minds off of a focus on what we don't have and place them squarely on what it is that we want and what we need to do or to have in place to get what we want. This is a benefit you get when residents understand the process of change. Educating and involving people in the process is the one way to help them develop the type of confidence they will need to manage and sustain the changes they will have helped to bring about.

Figure 8
THE THREE STAGES OF THE PROCESS

- **Stage 1 — Infrastructure Development:** This phase was considered complete on October 19, 2001. On that day College Hill hosted a presentation and site visit for the St. Louis Neighborhood Funders' Group (NFG). There were over 100 people assembled in the Bryan Hill Elementary School gymnasium for this meeting at 10:00 a.m. on a weekday. Since this phase involved the development of organization and communication capacity for the neighborhood, the fact that we were able to orchestrate such a visit in a two-week time frame revealed that it was in place and strong enough to identify and deliver *specific* resources that are needed to rebuild the community.[49]

▼

- **Stage 2 — Owner Occupied Housing Rehabilitation and Environmental Clean-up:** This phase will involve the rehabilitation of currently owned and occupied housing stock to Conservation District Code. Stage 2 officially began on October 20, 2001, the day after the NFG site visit. Stage 2 is the rehabilitation process that will focus mainly on homes that are owned and the primary residence of the owner. The process will also involve the rehabilitation of vacant homes that are structurally sound for rental and future ownership. The ultimate goal is to have a strong community that is anchored by 60% owner-occupied housing. We estimate that it will take us between six and eight years to finish the work of Stage 2.

▼

- **Stage 3 — New Home (In-fill) Construction and a Broad Talent Pool:** While the actual launching of Stage 3 is at least eight years away, we are in constant search for an organization or resource that has the structure, capacity and experience to help us. Given our goals for the overall redevelopment of the community, this organization will more than likely be faith-based because it will need to work very intimately with College Hill Community 2000, Inc. and the residents of the community. We have identified one organization that fits the general profile for our needs but discussions are very preliminary and we are too far from the completion of our objectives for Stage 2 to be actively involved with negotiations for Stage 3.

44 This notion was aptly expressed by Dr. Leonard Rubinowitz from Northwestern University as "Thought" and "Afterthought." Dr. Rubinowitz spoke as a panelist in February at the "Inequalities in Schools and Neighborhoods" conference held at Washington University. The "thought" is what you really care about and plan to do. It is where you put your best talent, thinking and your resources. The "afterthought" is the reaction to the unintended consequences that often arise as a response to the implementation of our "thoughts."

45 The primary elements and objectives of the College Hill Community Revitalization Process were articulated by a group of long-term residents at a community meeting in the summer of 1993. We have chosen to put our "thought" and expertise into achieving what they said they wanted.

46 The implied order or sequence in the steps of the strategy does not reflect the reality of our activities. In this type of development work, one finds that you have to work on all fronts at the same time.

47 In a paper entitled "What Happened to all the Money that was Designated for the Black Communities of North St. Louis," I document almost 30 years of development activity. Much of this activity was focused in the central corridor of the city but used programs and Federal resources that came to the city based upon the negative statistics that exist in the African American communities of North St. Louis.

48 A comparison of the heavy solid lines and the light dotted lines will delineate the difference between the resource acquisition strategy being pursued by College Hill Community 2000, Inc. from the traditional "outreach" approach for delivering resources and services to an underserved community.

49 This is one example of what we mean by the concept *incremental indicator of success*. The communications infrastructure was and is not as strong as it will need to be but it had to be in existence or such a meeting, given the short time frame, would not have been possible.

Appendix 6

TOWARD A MULTICULTURAL ORGANIZATION

By

Jarrow Merenivitch and Dan Reigle
Industrial Relations Division
THE PROCTER & GAMBLE COMPANY

TOWARD A MULTICULTURAL ORGANIZATION

This paper describes the evolution of organizations through Affirmative Action to the concept of effective multicultural management. It is designed to help the various Proctor & Gamble organizations and their managements to:

1. Assess where they are on the Affirmative Action continuum and set goals that will enable them to close the gap between where they are and where they want to be.

2. Design new organizations that will be able to capitalize fully on what has been learned about the dynamics of multicultural work forces.

3. Identify and manage the key multicultural issues facing Procter & Gamble now and in the future.

Beginning with a historical perspective, the paper analyzes the various stages in which organizations find themselves: the first generation of Affirmative Action, the second generation, and the truly multicultural phase.

For the purpose of this paper, a "multicultural organization" is defined as one that includes men and women, whites and ethnic minorities at various levels, and that effectively utilizes this diverse work force. Sex is specifically included as a cultural factor, since a person's gender has important cultural implications for the individuals's experiences, socialization, socially acceptable ranges of behavior, attitudes, work and life goals and expectations, and interests. There are other cultural factors — such as religion, socioeconomic status, age, language, physical handicaps, education, national or regional background — that also affect a person's acculturation within an organization and therefore should be considered in management situations. However, we are focusing here only on the two factors — race and gender — that have been examined the most extensively in organizational contexts.

The concepts presented here reflect the experiences over the past several years of a variety of organizations within Procter & Gamble. In an attempt to define some of the key principles learned through those experiences, Jarrow Merenivitch and Dan Reigle of P & G (Personnel Development Department) engaged with Dr. Price Cobbs of Pacific Management Systems in a series of intensive work sessions over a period of several months. This document is the product of those sessions.

Historical Background

From a historical perspective. Affirmative Action represents a societal response to organizational and institutionalized racism and sexism. It can be described as an attempt by organizations to increase the membership and participation of minorities and women. Prior to the implementation of Affirmative Action, organizations passed through two other stages:

1. **Stark Segregation.** This stage represented the obvious denial of opportunity to minorities and women. As recently as 1956, ads in the employment section of newspapers stated that Negroes should not apply; both minorities and women were segregated by custom and historical assumptions. Racial segregation was tolerated in most cases until the 1960s even though the armed services and federal agencies under the Truman Administration made attempts toward racial integration.

2. **Nondiscrimination.** As a result of the civil rights movement of the 1960s and early Equal Employment

> Opportunity legislation, a type of moral consciousness surfaced. This made it necessary for organizations to remove blatant evidence of discrimination, and advertisements began to carry the notation that "we do not discriminate on the basis of race, creed, color, or national origin." (Policies regarding gender were still largely unstated.) This nondiscrimination stage — vestiges of which can still be discerned in some of the nation's organizations — represented a passive approach which emphasized the removal of policies and activities that actively exclude the affected classes from employment. Therefore, it did not produce much change in organizational makeup. Women, white males, blacks, and other minority groups all received different treatment.

As a result of the lack of progress made under nondiscrimination policies, the federal government in the early 1970s began to require more proactivity in eliminating discrimination and its effects. U.S. organizations in general have now moved from passive nondiscrimination to Affirmative Action — the operative word being "action." The Affirmative Action stage can be divided into two sequential phases, or generations, characterized by different issues.

As organizational attention and energy are focused on resolving first generation issues, new issues tend to emerge and the organization moves into another phases of development — the second generation. The first and second generations of Affirmative Action are transition steps in the organizational evolution toward becoming an effective multicultural organization.

An organization's progression from first to second generation to multiculturalism is seldom divided into clear-cut steps; rather, the stages overlap and each stage will probably include some issues indicative of both earlier and later stages (see Figure 7).

The First Generation of Affirmative Action

When an organization is in the first phase of Affirmative Action, women and minorities are present in small percentages only, or occupy just the traditional roles — e.g., secretarial for women and heavy labor for blacks. The primary aim of organizations in the first generation is to comply with government regulations; there is little attempt to manage male/female or minority/white dynamics.

First-Generation Issues

1. ***Focus on Numbers.*** Numbers are the primary indicator used to determine whether additional organizational effort is needed.
   - The heaviest emphasis is on recruiting and on initial promotion of minorities and/or women from first level to second level.
   - Interpretation of numbers does not necessarily point toward organizational change. For example, high turnover among women and minorities is treated as an individual problem ("We need to hire better qualified women/minorities") rather than an organizational problem ("We lost two women managers out of four — does the organization need to change to improve this?").
   - Focus on numbers is often accompanied by rather superficial and/or short-term planning. For example, an organization may look at its needs for second-level minority managers in 1982, but not set up specific plans for getting there or identify the conditions and actions necessary to achieve the goals.
   - The numbers focus leads to fears and suspicions of reverse discrimination and potential charges and suits. For example, white employees who believe that meeting numerical goals for minority employees is the organizations's only concern are likely to believe that the organization will hire or promote any minority person just to meet the goal.

2. ***Crisis Orientation.*** Male/female or minority/white problems must be overt, visible, and serious in their implications before the organization is stimulated to act. An absence of such crises leads to a "why do anything?" syndrome, which is usually reinforced by the "numbers" orientation. The compliance/legal focus gauges need-for-action solely by the active crises or the suits and charges in process; "If we aren't getting EEO charges or open confrontations, we must be in an acceptable position." The organization's position is clearly reactive rather than proactive.

3. ***Resistance to Proactivity.*** There is a fear that proactivity will cause problems; to look at the problems will create (more, worse) problems. This situation is exacerbated if there is an unsupportive, skeptical organizational hierarchy to whom it is difficult to explain proactivity.

4. ***Social Issues.*** Problems may stem from unfamiliar relationships both inside and outside the office or plant. These new issues may include (a) housing for minorities in previously all-white neighborhoods; (b) tensions arising when men and women travel together on business; (c) accommodations in hotels and restaurants; (d) men and women, whites and minorities working together on irregular shifts where social needs are largely met in the work setting; (e) black managers' involvement in controversial community matters.

5. ***Racial and Sexual Hostility.*** Hostility of men toward women and of whites toward minorities is evident in racial slurs, sexual jokes, and open labeling or discounting. These incidents are not viewed by their perpetrators as racism or sexism. In fact, hostility is denied: "I didn't mean anything by that."

6. ***Trust.*** Unfamiliarity and newness of work relationships between whites and minorities, and between men and managerial level women, produce doubt and mistrust. For example, black managers perceive that they are being watched and tested by both management and black non-management employees as to where their "real" loyalties are.

7. ***Technical Competence.*** There is skepticism concerning the ability of minorities and women to succeed in some (if not all) types of positions or jobs. This is frequently the result of a deficit model applied to women and minority employees: women and minorities are assumed to be less capable than white males unless proved otherwise, and there is a feeling of surprise when a woman or minority person does in fact succeed.

   Also, black schools are not viewed as "good enough" preparation for certain positions. One result of these attitudes is that women and minorities tend to be retained in staff or support jobs longer than equally qualified white men before being given a line assignment. Another result is the creation of negative self-fulfilling prophecies.

8. ***Upward Mobility.*** The lack of women and minorities at upper levels of the organization and the effects of the deficit model operate to impose a perceived ceiling on their movement. White males are concerned that standards not be lowered for women and minorities. Little attention is given to the long-range utilization of women and minorities, with the result that they do not perceive much future for themselves beyond the second level.

9. ***Evaluation.*** In both hiring and performance appraisal situations, white male managers demonstrate — and often admit to — an inability to recognize and assess the real potential of minority and women employees. White male managers usually see groupings of minorities or women, as opposed to seeing a range of individuals with

different skills, styles, and capabilities. This often results in poor or non-existent performance feedback for women and minorities, or evaluation against purely subjective and varying criteria.

10. ***Involvement and Accountability.*** White males feel that the Personnel Department is responsible for Affirmative Action issues. In addition, Affirmative Action is not seen as a legitimate area for demonstration of managerial competence and potential. There is a mistrust or discounting of the motivation of white male managers involve din Affirmative Action ("I didn't know he was that liberal" or "What personal issues is he trying to push?"). The organization does not evaluate manages on the basis of their Affirmative Action performance. As a result of this combination of lack of rewards and performance standards plus some personal liabilities, white males do not identify their self-interest in Affirmative Action. Affirmative Action is extra-curricular for them.

11. ***Dual Roles.*** There is an expectation that black managers and women managers are all experts on Affirmative Action and that members of other minority groups are experts on their particular group. They are expected to educate others on the issues, provide a ready source of information, and serve as a pipeline to others. This dual role is typically not recognized as an additional job demand on women and minorities, an extra role that white male managers do not have.

12. ***Fear of Backlash.*** There is a pronounced fear of white male backlash. There is some justification for this: first, the focus on numbers creates a feeling that standards may be lowered and that minorities or women may be given unfair advantage because of their race or sex. Second, racial and gender problems are defined in the organization as "we/they" problems rather than "our" collec-

tive problems ("If Affirmative Action means that they are benefiting at my expense, then I will be resistant"). The fear of adverse reaction if offered at every step as a reason for not making a change forward greater equality of opportunity. Rather than confronting and managing the resistance to change, the organization slows down or stops Affirmative Action planning. "How fast can we go?" is a major concern.

13. ***Organizational Legitimacy.*** White male managers do not seriously believe that minorities and women constitute legitimate professional peers or competition for promotion. It is common to hear that women or minorities "have only made it because of Affirmative Action" or "wouldn't even be here if it weren't for the government." This attitude is reflected in assignments, performance appraisals, and the seriousness with which recommendations or reports from women and minorities are regarded. Because they are not taken seriously, minorities and women do not receive the information and support they need to carry out their responsibilities.

14. ***Sex and Color Blindness.*** One tendency is to deny that race and gender have anything to do with specific performance or interpersonal problems. Such inadequate problem definition results in poor solutions and in failure to take necessary action. For example:
    - When a black manager moves to a new plant in a white community, the organization ignores the potential effects on that manager's ability to find housing and takes no steps to head the problem off.
    - Resistance to a woman manager's authority is not taken into account in her performance reviews — even though she may be in charge of a crew that has never before had a woman manager.

15. ***Sex and Color Exaggeration*** At the other extreme, race

and gender are exaggerated as factors contributing to performance or interpersonal problems. For example, a conflict between a black employee and a white employee is viewed as solely caused by race, and other possible contributing factors are ignored. With such a narrow focus, the organization may fail to recognize general problems — such as inadequate training or career development programs — that affect others in the work force as well as the minorities and women.

16. ***Isolation of Affirmative Action.*** Affirmative Action is not a key focus area in organization-wide long-range planning and is not considered as an aspect of organizational development. As a result, Affirmative Action does not become as integral part of overall organizational goals and its potential as an agent for organizational change is not recognized.

The Second Generation of Affirmative Action

By the time an organization moves from the first generation of Affirmative Action to the second, it is usually meeting most of its numerical goals with regard to hiring women and minorities and is beginning to move away from a focus on compliance toward a focus on making the most of the heterogeneous nature of the organization. This does not mean that all of the first-generation problems are solved; many remain, although in subtler and/or more complex form. Others have been essentially resolved, but their resolution has given rise to new issues.

Second-Generation Issues

1. ***Critical Mass.*** The organization begins to consider how many women and minorities are needed at various levels to (1) provide a sufficient base of support, (2) offer a variety of role models and achievement patterns, (3) provide adequate articulation of Affirmative Action issues,

and (4) ensure individualization (for example, having enough black managers in the organization so that the fact that a manager is black is not the primary focus or dominant factor in work relationships). Plans are designed for achieving critical mass at different levels and in different sections of the organization.

2. ***"Racism and Sexism Are Dead."*** A prevalent assumption is that Affirmative Action problems are solved: "We've been cured and we're beyond that now." This attitude leads to complacency and inaction. In actuality, institutional and individual expressions of racism and sexism have not disappeared, but are taking less overt and hostile forms. Anxiety is still present, though it is likely to be denied.

3. ***Residual Stereotypes.*** White males are moving away from the "deficit model" orientation; they are better to perceive a range of minorities and women rather than seeing all minorities as a group or all women as a group. In some situations, however, stereotypes and negative assumptions still prevail. They usually stake a more subtle form than in the first generation — for example, doubting whether most minorities or women can succeed rather than expecting them to fail. Such attitudes are still capable of activating negative self-fulfilling prophecies.

4. ***Retention and Career Development.*** The organization is beginning to recognize that different things have happened to minorities and women, because of their race or sex, that have affected their career development. Once these issues are acknowledged, the organization must direct its problem-solving efforts toward minimizing the differential consequences. There is increasing concern about retaining high performing minorities and women and about developing them "fast enough," which replaces the first-generation concern over "whether we can hire enough who are qualified."

5. ***Career Disillusionment.*** Minorities and women feel increasing uncertainty and pessimism about their careers. At each level they find they have to deal with the same pressures to "prove themselves" that they faced at previous levels; they experience less power related to their roles than is available to white males; and they perceive ceilings on their advancement. As their disillusionment with the organization becomes evident, they are viewed as less motivated and less loyal, and their advancement becomes further threatened.

6. ***Implementing Accountability.*** It has become clear that Affirmative Action and the management of a diverse work force need to be "part of the job" and not an extracurricular activity for managers. It is recognized that white male managers' lack of ability to manage minorities and women can be viewed as managerial incompetence rather than a failure on the part of minorities and women to adapt to the organization. The issue now is how to ensure that inability or unwillingness to function effectively in a multicultural environment has negative career implications (as has inability to manage any other significant part of the business) and that multicultural management is a legitimate area for demonstrating competence and career potential (as are other key areas of the business).

7. ***Role of White Male Managers.*** White males in management have many questions regarding their role in Affirmative action, for example: How do I become a leader in Affirmative Action? How do I deal with the pressures from my own peers when I become proactive in Affirmative Action? Will I really be evaluated on the basis of how I deal with minorities as well as on how I carry out other responsibilities? How will this affect my future? What do racism and sexism cost me?

8. ***New Backlash Issues.*** As people experience changes in the organizational makeup, white males perceive threats to their own effectiveness and to their careers. Some feel that certain Affirmative Action programs give women and/or minorities an "unfair advantage." Thus, white males have begun to constitute an interest group whose needs must be considered. The organization becomes sensitive to actual or potential accusations of reverse discrimination.

9. ***Legitimate Discussion of Racial and Gender Issues.*** Racial and gender issues now have a legitimate place in boss-subordinate and other business discussions, but employees show differing skills and levels of comfort as they work in these areas. Although it is recognized that race and sex are potential contributing factors in performance and interpersonal problems, and that they are legitimate topics for investigation and discussion, the responsibility for opening such discussion still rests primarily with the women and minorities.

10. ***Constituency.*** The dual role of minorities and women, which surfaced in the first generation, is now recognized; but as minorities and women reach managerial levels, their burden increases rather than disappearing. It is not possible for a woman manager to steer clear of woman/man issues or for a black manager to steer clear of woman/man issues or for a black manager to avoid involvement in minority/white issues. Minority and female managers must constantly determine the level of their involvement in these issues — both within and outside their immediate work area. For example, they may need to decide whether to join a task force on Affirmative Action or how to respond to a request for counseling a woman or minority-group member in another part of the organization. In all of this, they are concerned with how they will be rewarded for their contributions in the area of Affirmative Action.

11. ***Racism vs. Sexism.*** In the first generation, the way an organization dealt with racial issues was the model for the way it dealt with gender issues, or vice versa. In the second generation, "dividing the pie" becomes an issue: How much effort and resources should be devoted to solving racism issues, and how much to solving sexism issues? Has Affirmative Action progress been unbalanced in favor of minorities or of women? Thus the victims of racism and sexism are pitted against each other.

12. ***Affirmative Action and Organizational Development.*** Rather than being thought of as a separate and distinct area of concern, Affirmative Action begins to be recognized as a stimulant of organizational change that goes beyond increasing the membership and participation of blacks and women. For example:

    - A program whose initial trust was to deal with the problems relating to career and skill development programs, performance appraisal and feedback, communications, and decision making. Solving these problems requires additional planning and resources but results in beneficial change for white males as well as for minorities and women.

    - An organization that has successfully implemented Affirmative Action programs finds itself in a much better position to deal with change of any sort. Learnings and skills are adaptable to other issues, such as major organizational changes, union-management relationships, selection and development of managers for both domestic and international assignments, and problems of older employees.

Figure 9
AFFIRMATIVE ACTION: FIRST AND SECOND GENERATIONS

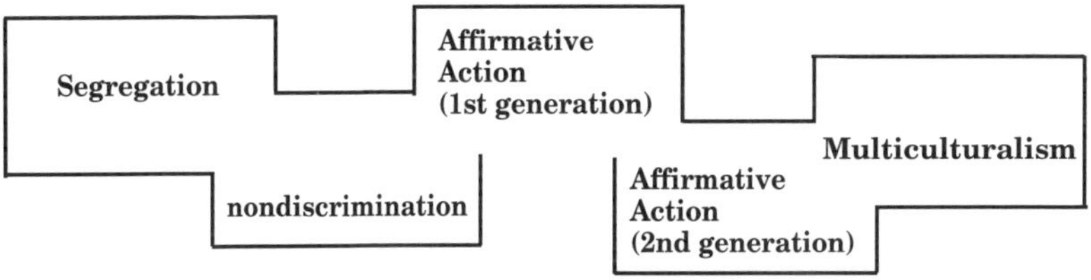

Figure 9 illustrates the progression of organizations from the stage of segregation to that of multiculturalism. The two generations of Affirmative Action are distinguished by the issues that prevail during each generation:

First Generation

- focus on numbers
- crisis orientation
- resistance to proactivity
- social issues
- racial & sexual hostility
- trust
- technical competence
- evaluation
- upward mobility
- involvement & accountability
- dual roles
- fear of backlash
- organizational legitimacy
- sex & color blindness
- sex & color exaggeration
- isolation of Affirmative Action

Second Generation

- critical mass
- "racism & sexism are dead"
- residual stereotypes
- retention & career development
- career disillusionment
- implementing accountability
- role of white male managers
- new backlash issues
- legitimate discussion of racial & sexual issues
- constituency
- racism vs. sexism
- Affirmative Action and organizational development

Principles for Design and Development of Multicultural Organizations

An organization that has reached the second generation of Affirmative Action has a diverse work force that is, its employees differ in race, sex and ethnic background. Most organizations today have or soon will have diverse work forces; it is no longer acceptable, feasible, or economically productive to start up or perpetuate an organization with an all-white/all-male work force and culture.

Organizational Criteria

An organization that operates effectively in utilizing its diverse work force can be described as a multicultural organization. A diverse work force does not in itself constitute a multicultural organization, for a true multicultural organization has several other distinguishing characteristics (based on concepts developed by Dr. Robert W. Terry):

- It actively seeks to capitalize on the advantages of its diversity — rather than attempting to stifle or ignore the diversity — and to minimize the barriers that can develop as a result of people having different backgrounds, attitudes, values, behavior styles, and concerns.
- Organizational resources (key jobs, income, prerequisites, access to information, etc.) are distributed equitably and are not determined or affected by cultural characteristics such as race or sex.
- The ability to influence decisions and the way they are carried out is shared widely, not differentially by cultural characteristics.
- The organizational culture (assumptions about people and groups, take-it-for-granted norms, the way work gets done) is pluralistic in that it recognizes and appreciates diversity; it acknowledges both the need for "being the same" in some ways to work together effectively and the need for "being different" in some ways to recognize in-

dividual and group interests, concerns and backgrounds.
- Institutional policies, practices, and procedures are flexible and responsive to the needs of all employees.

Multicultural status is the goal toward which organizations are striving as they move through the first and second generations of Affirmative Action. A true multicultural organization is achieved by applying the following principles:

1. ***Heterogeneity.*** We live in a culturally pluralistic society, and the organization's employees are products of that society. All groups making up the organization must be seen as integral parts of it, rather than "extra" groups that have been added on. Diversity must be recognized and managed, rather than ignored, and must be viewed as providing opportunities to be utilized rather than headaches to be tolerated or avoided.

2. ***People as Individuals and as Group Members.*** Every person is an individual with a unique set of strengths, weaknesses, and needs. To deal with each other on the basis of accurate information, we must be able to perceive others in the work force as a range of individuals rather than as groups distinguished by race, sex, or other characteristics; to avoid making sweeping (usually negative) generalizations and assumptions about the abilities and personality traits of others, and to take advantage of the special skills and abilities that each person contributes.

   At the same time, the race, sex, and other groups to which individuals belong often affect their experiences, other people's expectations of them, the way they are dealt with, the pressures on them, and their job performance. Therefore, in order to take advantage of the diversity of its work force, a multicultural organization must utilize a *dual focus;* viewing individuals as unique and also recognizing the effects of cultural background on work effectiveness. Support groups (such as black managers' groups) may be helpful in enabling the organization to develop the second focus. Such groups provide opportunities for individuals to share experiences, identify norms and patterns, develop skills for dealing with their situations, and re-examine areas that may need to be changed.

3. ***Shared Responsibility.*** Maintaining the effectiveness of the multicultural organization is a responsibility shared by everyone in the organization. All employees must be actively involve in a continuing review and refinement of organizational norms, climate, practices, and patterns of behavior so that they will be supportive of the goals of a multicultural organization. White males must be proactive, not relying solely on women and minorities to define issues and problem areas.

   Shared responsibility also has implications for behavioral change. For example, as women participate in management, both men and women will be required to make some changes — i.e., some women may need to develop new outlooks on career building and leadership, while men may need to develop the ability to deal with women in professional, business roles. Pressure to make such changes is not placed disproportionately on women or minorities within the organization.

   The principle of shared responsibility requires that the organization *formally declare* that no groups will be victimized or left out, and that addressing the needs felt by some sub-group will strengthen the entire organization.

4. ***Deliberate, Planned Change.*** Building an effective multicultural organization is an effort that must be planned and managed in much the same manner as any other major aspect of the business. It will not "just happen" without management attention and resources. As-

pects of this principle include the following:

(a) A new production module or department, progressing through startup to normal operations, does not do so in "one great leap," but in a series of smaller steps. Similarly, an organization cannot move from all-white/all male work force to diverse work force to multicultural organization in one jump. Instead, there will be separate phases in the development process, each of which must be analyzed, planned, and managed in order to move on successfully to the next phase.

(b) Just as equipment requires periodic preventive maintenance, a multicultural organization requires periodic reviews involving the entire social system and its progress in becoming multicultural. Such maintenance is necessary to keep the system on track toward its goals, to continually refine objectives, and to keep goal-directed energy at a level sufficient to produce results.

(c) The information needed to accomplish (a) and (b) above must be complete and accurate in order to measure progress and identify needs for corrective action. This requires that methods and systems be designed and used to collect and analyze information about the functioning of the organization.

(d) Commitment of resources (time, money, people) must accompany the planning of the changes. Without resources, the work needed to move the organization ahead will not get done. Further, people often "read" the level of importance accorded a project by the type and level of resources devoted to it.

5. ***Problem Definition.*** To make work force diversity a positive asset in the organization, the viewpoint used to look at problems is important. The approach to the problem determines the range of available actions or solutions,

the extent to which the organization's problem-solving capability can be used, and the extent to which problems can be turned into opportunities.

Problems that arise as a result of work force diversity need to be defined as organizational and management problems rather than women's problems or minorities' problems; as business problems, not protest group issues to be settled outside the organization; as "our" collective problems, not "we vs. they" problems; and as opportunities for strengthening the social system of the organization, not as irritants to be ignored or addressed with minimal efforts until they explode.

Problem definition is a critical factor in the relationship of the organization to its women and minority employees. For example, failing to pay attention to problems that particularly affect black managers increases the personal load on those managers and may build a perception that the organization does not value their contribution or continued participation. It may build a sense that they are "outsiders" and cause reduced commitment to the organization and its goals.

6. ***Problem Analysis.*** In a multicultural organization, people must be able to analyze performance or interpersonal problems in terms of *both* cultural factors and other types of actors. That is, people and the organization as a whole must avoid both sex/color blindness and sex/color exaggeration. This requires increased penetration of problems before action is taken.

7. ***Self-interest.*** The organization must define how being multicultural helps it meet its business and quality-of-work-life objectives and goals. What problems does it help the organization solve or avoid? What opportunities does it present that may be capitalized upon? A primary function of leadership is to enable employees to understand

how and why the movement toward multiculturalism is important to the organization, and to identify with their roles and responsibilities in making it happen.

8. ***Accountability.*** Accountability means being responsible for achieving results, for making things happen. Managers in a multicultural organization must be held accountable for initiating, direction, and controlling the processes that help to make individuals and groups effective in achieving multicultural goals and objectives. All members of the organization must be clearly accountable for:
   (a) understanding the nature of multicultural organizations,
   (b) contributing to the implementation, effectiveness, and maintenance of the organization as a multicultural system, and
   (c) adjusting their personal behaviors and skills to meet the requirements for working effectively in a multicultural environment.

Management Criteria

The success of managers in a multicultural organization — which operates on the basis of the above principles — is tied to their ability to achieve results. Certain characteristics are shared by managers who are effective in a multicultural organization, and these characteristics must be considered in assignment decisions, performance evaluation, salary reviews, developmental and training opportunities, and career planning.

An effective multicultural manager:

- Actively seeks to learn from his/her and others' experiences and to improve as a manager in a multicultural organization.
- Has established a personal perspective on multicultural management, viewing it as a challenge, an opportunity,

and something to be mastered rather than as a set of problems.

- Is sensitive to and knowledgeable about the issues that commonly arise in diverse work forces; takes initiative in averting potential problems and solving existing ones.
- Has a high capacity for examination of thoughts, feelings, attitudes, and beliefs about race, sex, or people who are different on any cultural dimension; actively examines personally held assumptions, taking care not to view differences among people as indications that some of those people are inferior or strange; always works to understand help others understand the impact of such assumptions on individual's job performance and overall organizational results.
- Seeks to place perceptions and discussions of race, sex, and other factors into a rational framework by seeking out facts and substituting factual information for myths and stereotypes.
- Establishes discussions of race, sex, and other cultural factors as legitimate aspects of problem analysis, decision making, and other areas of organizational life.
- Seeks out skills, traits, and characteristics that may be unrecognized or undervalued and finds ways to convert these new potentials into higher productivity and contributions. This involves a willingness to commit time and energy to assessing needs and capitalizing on opportunities.